Advanced Hybrid Frameworks for Aspect-Level Sentiment Analytics

AF867707

Keneddy Frown

LIST OF CONTENTS

CHAPTER 1

INTRODUCTION

Background

"Research is essentially an investigation, a recording and an analysis of evidence for the purpose of gaining knowledge"

- Robert Ross.

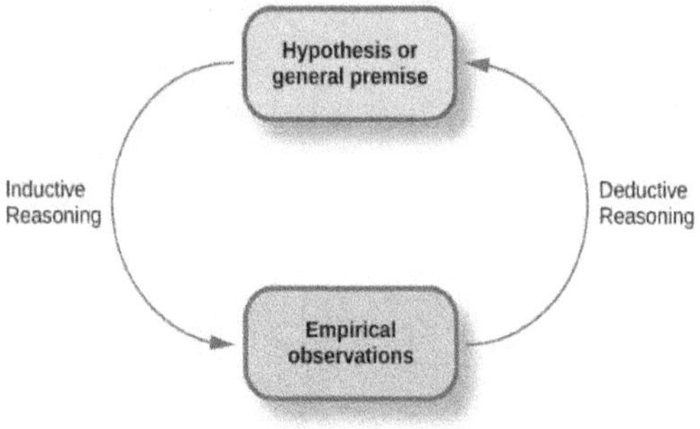

This chapter lays a solid groundwork for exploring predictive modeling in the context of fine-grained sentiment analysis. It begins by situating Sentiment Analysis (SA) within the broader domain of Natural Language Processing (NLP), then transitions into a focused discussion on Fine-Grained Sentiment Analysis (FSA), emphasizing its unique attributes. The chapter clearly defines the central research problem and articulates the primary objectives guiding the study. It outlines the research methodology employed and provides a general overview of the investigation. Finally, the chapter concludes by presenting the structure of the thesis and offering a concise summary

1.1 Introduction

Sentiment Analysis (SA), often referred to as opinion mining, is a crucial subfield within the broader domain of Natural Language Processing (NLP)[1]. NLP is a branch of artificial intelligence that enables computers to understand, interpret, and generate human language. Within this framework, SA focuses specifically on identifying and extracting the emotional tone, sentiment, or subjective information expressed in text. It allows us to automatically determine whether a piece of writing—be it a review, tweet, article, or any other textual data— expresses a positive, negative, or neutral sentiment, or even more nuanced emotions. By applying NLP techniques, SA processes and analyzes human language to uncover the underlying opinions and attitudes, making it an invaluable tool for understanding public perception, customer feedback, and social media trends.[2]

1.1.1 Understanding Sentiment Analysis

Sentiment Analysis (SA), often referred to as opinion mining, is a specialized task within Natural Language Processing (NLP) that focuses on identifying and extracting subjective information from text. It aims to determine the emotional tone conveyed in written or spoken language—classifying it as positive, negative, neutral, or even more nuanced emotions such as joy, anger, or sadness. SA plays a pivotal role in interpreting human expression in digital communication. Whether analysing customer reviews, social media posts, or news articles, SA helps uncover public opinion, emotional reactions, and behavioral patterns.[3] In human communication, emotions are conveyed through spoken words, facial expressions, and gestures, allowing for effective emotional exchange [1]. Machines, however, must simulate this capability by capturing, processing, and expressing emotions using multimodal learning [2]. With the growth of social media, multimodal sentiment analysis (MSA) has emerged as a crucial approach, integrating audio, video, and text to enhance sentiment prediction [3]. Despite improvements in fusion techniques like tensor-based models, overcoming modality gaps remains a challenge in this field [4].

Multimodal data comprises distinct types of information, and the synergy between text and images offers a more complete emotional perspective [5]. Visual elements can strengthen emotion recognition in textual content. One of the key challenges in Multimodal Aspect-Based Sentiment Analysis (MABSA) is extracting and interpreting visual features effectively, as they are essential for nuanced sentiment analysis [6]. Another critical issue in multimodal processing after feature extraction is ensuring meaningful interaction between data sources. Haphazard fusion of unrelated elements can cause misalignment and loss of valuable information [7]. Simply merging data without consideration may fail to exploit the advantages of each modality, potentially distorting insights [8]. However, strategically aligning related information through semantic connections can enhance the overall analytical value of the data [9].

A complete interpretation of an image relies on the connection and balance between local and global information. Understanding this structure enhances precision in content recognition while deepening the grasp of complex contexts and semantic depth [10]. For example, a cheerful expression on a person's face often corresponds with a festive event or a picturesque backdrop, collectively conveying a sense of joy [11]. Likewise, embedded text within an image acts as additional context, strengthening the overall message and emotion. A rainy day image paired with melancholic text, for instance, heightens the feeling of gloom [12].

SA builds upon core NLP techniques to transform raw text into sentiment insights:

Table 1.1: NLP Pipeline

NLP Stage	Role in Sentiment Analysis
Text Preprocessing	Cleans and prepares text (tokenization, stop-word removal)
Feature Extraction	Converts text into numerical form (TF-IDF, word embeddings)
Sentiment Classification	Applies models to predict sentiment (SVM, LSTM, BERT)
Output Interpretation	Presents sentiment scores or labels (e.g., positive/negative)

The Natural Language Processing (NLP) pipeline is a structured sequence of steps that transforms raw linguistic data into meaningful insights. It begins with data acquisition, where textual information is gathered from sources such as websites, social media, or documents. This is followed by text cleaning, which removes noise like HTML tags, special characters, and spelling errors to ensure data quality. Next comes text preprocessing, involving techniques such as tokenization, stop-word removal, stemming, and lemmatization—essential for breaking down language into analyzable units. Once the text is prepared, feature extraction converts it into numerical representations using methods like Bag-of-Words, TF-IDF, or word embeddings[7]. These features are then fed into machine learning or deep learning models for tasks such as classification, sentiment detection, or entity recognition. The final stages include evaluation, where model performance is assessed using metrics like accuracy and F1-score, and deployment, which integrates the model into real-world applications such as Chabot, recommendation systems, or sentiment analysis tools. This pipeline ensures that unstructured text is systematically processed into structured, actionable knowledge.

1.1.2 Evolution of Sentiment Analysis

Sentiment analysis has evolved significantly over time, moving from simpler rule- based and lexicon-based methods to more sophisticated machine learning and deep learning techniques. Initially, sentiment analysis relied on predefined linguistic rules and sentiment dictionaries to classify text as positive, negative, or neutral. While straightforward, these methods often struggled with context and nuance. The introduction of machine learning marked a major shift. Supervised learning methods like Support Vector Machines (SVM), Naïve Bayes, and decision trees were trained on labelled datasets to predict sentiments in new text, offering greater flexibility and accuracy. More recently, deep learning has revolutionized the field with models capable of capturing intricate patterns and dependencies in text. Techniques such as Long Short-Term Memory (LSTM) networks, Convolutional Neural Networks (CNNs), and Transformer-based models (e.g., BERT) have demonstrated superior performance in sentiment analysis, processing large amounts of data and learning complex representations that enhance accuracy. This evolution has made sentiment analysis increasingly important in various industries, including e-commerce, healthcare, and customer service, where understanding user sentiments can drive better decision-making and improve user experiences. As mentioned, the journey began with rule-based and lexicon-based methods. These relied on handcrafted rules and pre-compiled dictionaries of words with associated sentiment scores. For example, a rule might state that the presence of words like "great," "excellent," or "love" indicates positive sentiment, while "terrible," "bad," or "hate" suggests negative sentiment. While simple and interpretable, these methods were often rigid and struggled to capture the nuances of human language, such as sarcasm, irony, or context-dependent meanings. The advent of machine learning brought a significant leap forward. Instead of relying on fixed rules, ML models learned from large datasets of text labelled with their corresponding sentiments. Algorithms like Support Vector Machines (SVM), Naïve Bayes, and decision trees became popular choices. These models could identify complex patterns and relationships between words and sentiments that were difficult to capture with rule-based approaches. This allowed for greater flexibility and adaptability to different domains and types of text. The most recent and impactful stage in the evolution is the rise of deep learning. Deep learning models, particularly those based on neural networks, have the ability to learn hierarchical representations of text, capturing intricate dependencies and contextual information. Techniques like Long Short-Term Memory (LSTM) networks are well-suited for processing sequential data like text, enabling them to remember information from previous words and understand the overall sentiment of a sentence or document. Convolutional Neural Networks (CNNs) can identify local patterns and features in text, which can be useful for tasks like aspect-based sentiment analysis. More recently, Transformer-based models like BERT have achieved state-of-the-art performance by leveraging attention mechanisms to capture long-range dependencies and contextual relationships in text. This continuous evolution has led to more accurate, robust, and versatile sentiment analysis systems that can handle a wider range of text data and provide deeper insights into human sentiments.

Natural Language Processing (NLP) confronts the intricate subtleties of human language, skilfully navigating the complexities of slang, idiomatic expressions, and cultural nuances. At its core, NLP promotes inclusivity by bridging linguistic divides and amplifying diverse voices. It serves as the technological cornerstone that enables machines to comprehend, interact, and respond empathetically within the human Linguistic sphere—a dynamic convergence of linguistics, data science, and artificial intelligence that fosters deeper understanding and connection. Within this framework, sentiment analysis operates in close synergy with NLP. While NLP provides the structural and semantic foundation, sentiment analysis builds upon it to interpret emotional undertones embedded in text. Together, they form a powerful alliance that continually advances our ability to unravel the rich and layered fabric of human expression, revealing insights that lie beneath the surface of everyday communication Sentiment analysis, the emotional virtuoso, specializes in uncovering the sentiments and opinions buried within textual data. It takes the language understanding abilities bestowed by NLP and directs them toward the profound task of gauging human emotions. Like a skilled interpreter, sentiment analysis deciphers the emotional melody of words, determining whether the sentiment is positive, negative, or neutral. Together, NLP and sentiment analysis form a dynamic duo. As a language Comprehension, NLP provides the foundation for understanding the linguistic structure and context of text. Sentiment analysis leverages this understanding to discern emotional tones, ensuring that the sentiment classification considers the subtleties of language. For feature Extraction, NLP identifies relevant features in text, such as keywords, entities, and grammatical structures. Sentiment analysis utilizes these features to extract sentiment-bearing words or phrases, allowing for more accurate sentiment classification.

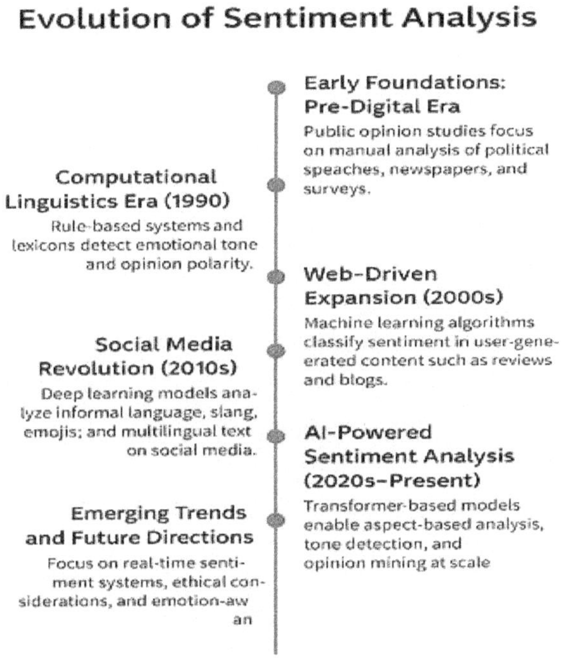

Figure 1.1: Evolution of sentiment Analysis

1.2 Natural Language Processing

Natural Language Processing (NLP) engages with the intricate subtleties of human language, skilfully navigating the complexities of slang, idioms, and cultural nuances. It champions inclusivity by breaking down linguistic barriers and ensuring that every voice is acknowledged. At its core, NLP is a powerful fusion of linguistics, data science, and artificial intelligence—an enabling force that allows machines to comprehend, communicate, and even empathize through language. In this symphony of understanding, NLP and Sentiment Analysis (SA) perform in harmony, each enhancing the other's capabilities. NLP lays the foundational framework for language comprehension, equipping machines with the tools to interpret and generate text. It encompasses essential techniques such as syntax analysis, part-of- speech tagging, named entity recognition, and semantic parsing—all of which serve as the building blocks for sentiment analysis. SA, in turn, focuses on the emotional dimension of language, uncovering the sentiments and opinions embedded within textual data[20]. Like a skilled interpreter, it translates the emotional undertones of words, classifying them as positive, negative, or neutral. Together, NLP and SA form a dynamic partnership. In terms of linguistic comprehension, NLP provides the structural and contextual understanding necessary for accurate sentiment detection[32]. For feature extraction, NLP identifies key elements such as entities, keywords, and grammatical patterns, which SA then uses to isolate sentiment- bearing expressions. When it comes to contextual interpretation, NLP excels at grasping the broader meaning of text, enabling SA to detect subtle cues like sarcasm or irony that would otherwise be missed. Their collaboration extends beyond text, offering multimodal insights by integrating NLP's textual analysis with other data types such as images and audio. This synergy powers a wide range of applications—from social media monitoring and customer feedback analysis to market research and brand reputation management. By working together, NLP and SA help organizations decode public sentiment, make informed decisions, and respond with greater empathy and precision.

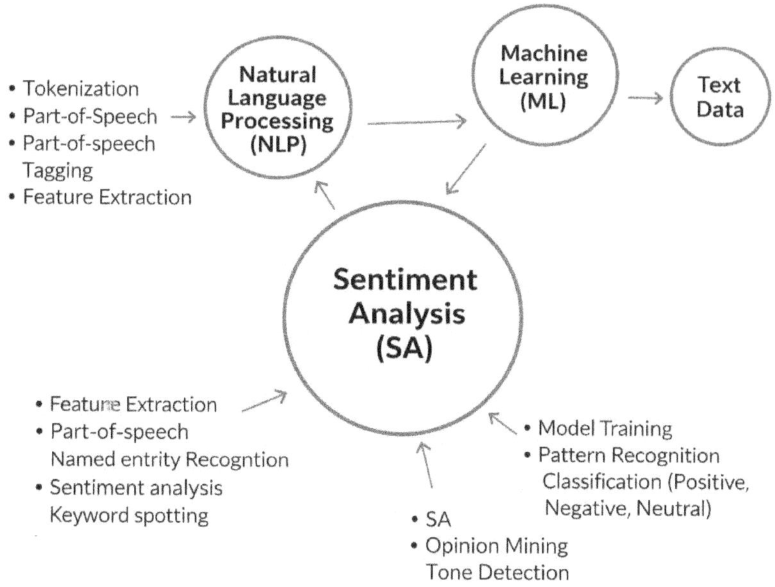

Figure 1.2: SA using ML and NLP

The integration of Natural Language Processing (NLP) and Machine Learning (ML) forms a powerful alliance in the realm of Sentiment Analysis (SA). This partnership is not merely complementary—it is deeply interdependent. NLP provides the linguistic structure and semantic understanding necessary to interpret human language, while ML contributes the adaptive intelligence required to learn patterns and make accurate predictions. Together, they enable machines to decode emotional content with increasing precision.

NLP acts as the linguistic architect, equipping systems with the ability to process and understand text through techniques such as syntax analysis, part-of-speech tagging, named entity recognition, and semantic parsing. These foundational tools allow ML models to work with structured, meaningful data. ML, in turn, serves as the predictive engine, training on labelled datasets to classify sentiment and refine its accuracy over time.

Sentiment Analysis emerges from this fusion as a specialized task that interprets the emotional tone of text. It leverages NLP's structural insights and ML's pattern recognition to determine whether a message conveys positive, negative, or neutral sentiment. This collaboration extends across multiple layers of analysis—from identifying sentiment-bearing phrases to understanding context, such as sarcasm or irony, which would be difficult to detect without NLP's deeper linguistic comprehension.

Moreover, this synergy supports multimodal applications, where SA can analyze text alongside images or audio by drawing on NLP's ability to interpret accompanying captions or transcripts. In practical terms, the fusion of NLP and ML powers a wide range of real-world applications, including social media monitoring, customer feedback analysis, market research, and brand reputation management. By working in tandem, NLP and ML enable organizations to extract meaningful emotional insights from language, guiding data-driven decisions and fostering more empathetic engagement with users[8].

1.3 Sentiment Analysis Process

The diagram illustrates a structured workflow for conducting fine-grained sentiment analysis, comprising five sequential stages. The process begins with Data Collection, where relevant textual data is gathered from sources such as social media, customer reviews, or survey responses. This raw data then undergoes Preprocessing, which involves cleaning and preparing the text—removing noise, tokenizing, normalizing, and handling linguistic variations—to ensure consistency and quality [13].

Next, the Feature Extraction stage transforms the pre-processed text into numerical representations using techniques such as TF-IDF, word embeddings, or syntactic patterns. These features serve as input for Sentiment Classification, where machine learning or deep learning models are employed to determine the sentiment polarity or emotional tone of the text. Finally, the output is refined through Fine-Grained Sentiment Analysis, which goes beyond basic polarity detection to capture nuanced sentiments, such as specific emotions or aspect- based evaluations. This layered approach enables a deeper understanding of human expression and supports more accurate and context-aware sentiment interpretation.

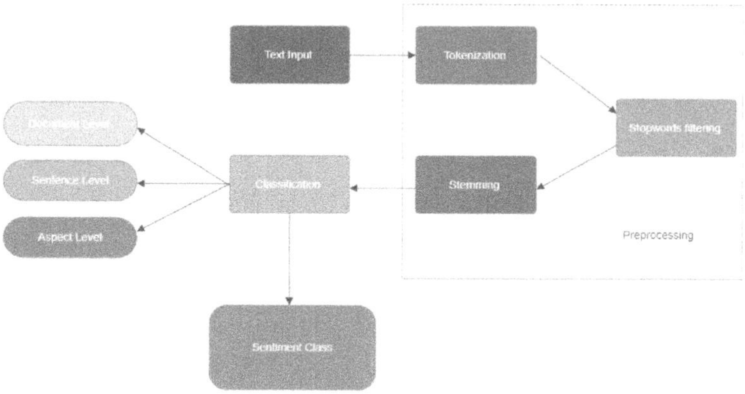

Figure 1.3: Sentiment Analysis Process

1.4 Research Problem

In human communication, emotions are conveyed through spoken words, facial expressions, and gestures, allowing for effective emotional exchange. With the growth of social media, multimodal sentiment analysis (MSA) has emerged as a crucial approach, integrating text, image and audio to enhance sentiment prediction. As it is static system model Despite improvements in fusion techniques like tensor-based models, overcoming modality gaps remains a challenge in this field. Multimodal data comprises distinct types of information, and the synergy between text and images offers a more complete emotional perspective.

1.4.1 Motivation

In an era where digital communication dominates personal, commercial, and social interactions, understanding the emotional undertones embedded in textual data has become increasingly vital. Traditional sentiment analysis, which classifies text into broad categories such as positive, negative, or neutral, often fails to capture the nuanced expressions and contextual subtleties inherent in human language. Fine-grained sentiment analysis addresses this limitation by offering a more detailed and precise interpretation of sentiment, including intensity levels, aspect-specific evaluations, and emotion classification. This granularity is particularly valuable in domains such as customer feedback, social media monitoring, healthcare narratives, and political discourse, where subtle shifts in sentiment can signal emerging trends, user satisfaction, or public opinion. By enabling a deeper understanding of textual sentiment, fine-grained analysis enhances decision-making, fosters empathetic AI systems, and contributes to more inclusive and responsive language technologies.

1.4.2 Problem Definition

While traditional sentiment analysis has proven effective in categorizing text into broad sentiment classes—such as positive, negative, or neutral—it often overlooks the nuanced emotional expressions and contextual dependencies embedded in natural language. This limitation becomes particularly pronounced in domains where sentiment is multifaceted, aspect-specific, or influenced by cultural and linguistic subtleties. Fine- grained sentiment analysis (FSA) seeks to address these challenges by offering a more detailed interpretation of sentiment, including intensity levels, aspect-based evaluations, and emotion classification. However, achieving this granularity requires sophisticated modeling techniques capable of capturing semantic richness, contextual cues, and implicit sentiment indicators. The core problem addressed in this study is the development of an effective predictive modeling framework for fine-grained sentiment analysis that balances interpretability, accuracy, and adaptability across diverse textual datasets. To achieve this problem Develop a multimodal sentiment analysis framework that fuses text, image, and audio signals to predict fine-grained sentiment labels more reliably than single-modal baselines.

1.4.3 Challenges Associated with Research Problem

Fine-grained sentiment analysis presents a range of complex challenges that extend beyond traditional sentiment classification. One of the primary difficulties lies in accurately capturing the subtle emotional nuances and contextual dependencies embedded in natural language. Sentiment is often expressed implicitly, through sarcasm, idioms, or culturally specific references, making it difficult for models to interpret without deep contextual understanding. Additionally, aspect-based sentiment analysis requires precise identification and disambiguation of entities or features within text, which can be hindered by noisy data, domain variability, and linguistic ambiguity. The scarcity of annotated datasets for fine-grained sentiment categories further complicates model training and evaluation.

Moreover, balancing model performance with interpretability remains a persistent challenge, especially when deploying deep learning architectures that function as black boxes. These issues collectively underscore the need for robust, adaptable, and transparent predictive frameworks capable of handling the intricacies of fine-grained sentiment analysis across diverse textual environments.

1.5 Research

Objectives Aim

The primary aim of this research is to develop a robust and interpretable predictive modeling framework for fine-grained sentiment analysis that effectively captures nuanced emotional expressions, aspect-specific sentiments, and contextual dependencies within natural language texts.

Objectives

1. To investigate the limitations of traditional sentiment analysis approaches in handling subtle and context-dependent sentiment expressions.
2. To design and implement a hybrid modeling framework that integrates linguistic rules, lexicon-based methods, and deep learning architectures for fine-grained sentiment detection.
3. To explore the effectiveness of contextual embeddings (e.g., BERT) in capturing semantic and emotional nuances across diverse textual domains.
4. To evaluate the proposed framework using benchmark datasets and performance metrics such as precision, recall, F1-score, and interpretability.
5. To demonstrate the applicability of the model in real-world scenarios such as customer feedback analysis, social media monitoring, and domain-specific sentiment tracking.

Scope

This research focuses on the development and evaluation of a predictive modeling framework for fine-grained sentiment analysis within the domain of Natural Language Processing. Emphasis on aspect-level sentiment detection and emotion classification. Evaluation of model performance using standard NLP benchmarks. Exclusion of multimodal sentiment analysis (e.g., image or video-based sentiment) and non-English language corpora.

1.5.1 Research Plan

To achieve the objectives stated above the following tasks have been conducted:

Literature Review

Conduct a comprehensive review of existing approaches to sentiment analysis and fine-grained sentiment modelling. Identify gaps in current methodologies, especially in aspect-level and emotion-specific sentiment detection. Analyze the evolution of NLP techniques relevant to sentiment interpretation.

Problem Formulation and Dataset Selection

Define the research problem and hypotheses based on insights from the literature. Select or construct suitable datasets for fine-grained sentiment analysis (e.g., product reviews, social media posts). Ensure datasets include aspect-level annotations or emotional labels where applicable.

Methodology Design

Develop a hybrid modeling framework combining rule-based, lexicon-based, and deep learning techniques. Integrate contextual embeddings (e.g., BERT) and attention mechanisms to capture nuanced sentiment. Design preprocessing and feature extraction pipelines tailored to fine-grained tasks.

Model Implementation and Training

Implement the proposed models using appropriate tools and libraries (e.g., Python, PyTorch, Tensor-Flow).Train models on selected datasets and fine-tune parameters for optimal performance. Apply techniques such as transfer learning and data augmentation to enhance generalizability.

Evaluation and Validation

Evaluate model performance using metrics such as precision, recall, F1-score, and aspect-level accuracy. Compare results with baseline models to demonstrate improvements. Conduct error analysis to identify limitations and refine the approach.

Interpretation and Visualization

Use explain ability tools to interpret model decisions Visualize sentiment trends, aspect distributions, and emotional intensities using graphs and dashboards.

Documentation and Thesis Writing

Compile findings, methodologies, and results into structured thesis chapters. Reflect on the implications of the research and propose future directions. Ensure academic rigor, clarity, and coherence throughout the documentation.

Model Implementation and Training

Implement the proposed models using appropriate tools and libraries (e.g., Python, PyTorch, and Tensor Flow). Train models on selected datasets and fine-tune parameters for optimal performance. Apply techniques such as transfer learning and data augmentation to enhance generalizability.

Evaluation and Validation

Evaluate model performance using metrics such as precision, recall, F1-score, and aspect-level accuracy. Compare results with baseline models to demonstrate improvements. Conduct error analysis to identify limitations and refine the approach.

Interpretation and Visualization

Use explain ability tools to interpret model decisions. Visualize sentiment trends, aspect distributions, and emotional intensities using graphs and dashboards.

1.6 Thesis Organization

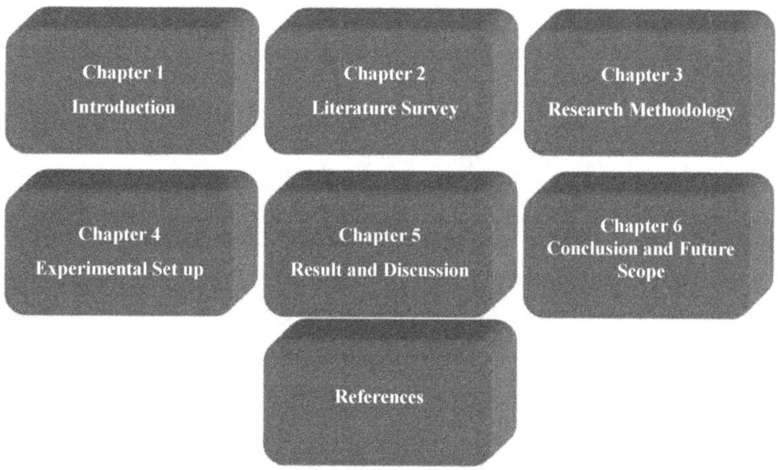

Chapter 1: Introduction

This chapter introduces the research topic, highlighting the growing importance of sentiment analysis in understanding human emotions and opinions expressed through text. It outlines the limitations of traditional sentiment classification methods and motivates the need for fine-grained approaches that capture subtle, context-dependent sentiments. The chapter presents the research aim, objectives, scope, and significance, establishing the foundation for the study.

Chapter 2: Literature Review

This chapter provides a comprehensive review of existing work in sentiment analysis, including lexicon-based methods, machine learning models, and deep learning architectures. It critically examines prior studies on aspect-based sentiment analysis, emotion classification, and contextual embeddings. The review identifies key gaps in current methodologies, particularly in handling implicit sentiment and linguistic nuance, thereby justifying the proposed research direction.

Chapter 3: Research Methodology

This chapter outlines the methodological framework adopted for the study. It details the hybrid approach integrating linguistic rules, lexicon-based techniques, and deep learning models such as BERT. The chapter describes the data sources, preprocessing steps, feature extraction methods, and model architecture. It also explains the rationale behind the chosen techniques and how they align with the research objectives.

Chapter 4: Dataset Construction and Experimental Setup

This chapter focuses on the creation and preparation of the dataset used for fine-grained sentiment analysis. It describes the data collection process, cleaning procedures, annotation strategies, and aspect-level tagging. The experimental setup, including training configurations, hyper-parameter tuning, and evaluation protocols, is also presented to ensure reproducibility and transparency.

Chapter 5: Results and Evaluation

This chapter presents the empirical findings of the study. It reports the performance of the proposed model using metrics such as precision, recall, F1-score, and interpretability scores. Comparative analysis with baseline models is conducted to demonstrate the effectiveness of the hybrid framework. The chapter also includes error analysis and visualizations to highlight model strengths and limitations.

Chapter 6: Conclusion and Future Work

This final chapter summarizes the key contributions of the research, reaffirming the value of fine-grained sentiment analysis in advancing NLP capabilities. It revisits the research objectives and highlights how they were addressed. The chapter concludes with suggestions for future work, including expanding to multilingual datasets, incorporating multimodal sentiment cues, and enhancing model transparency.

CHAPTER 2

REVIEW OF LITERATURE

Background Ideology and Review of Literature:

While traditional sentiment analysis has made significant strides in classifying emotional polarity at the document or sentence level, it often lacks the granularity required to understand sentiments directed toward specific components or attributes of an entity. The present study aims to address this gap by proposing a robust framework for Aspect-Based Sentiment Analysis using Attention Mechanisms integrated with Multimodal Data. By combining linguistic precision with cross-modal emotional cues, the research seeks to enhance the interpretability, accuracy, and domain adaptability of sentiment analysis systems particularly any sensitive contexts.

2.1 Sentiment Analysis

With the explosion of digital content across social media, customer reviews, and online forums, sentiment analysis has become essential for extracting meaningful insights from vast volumes of unstructured data. It plays a critical role in domains such as business intelligence, healthcare, politics, and disaster response. Early approaches relied on traditional machine learning algorithms like Naive Bayes and Support Vector Machines, often using handcrafted features and sentiment lexicons. However, recent advancements have shifted toward deep learning models, especially transformer-based architectures like BERT, which offer superior contextual understanding and adaptability across languages and domains. Despite its progress, sentiment analysis faces ongoing challenges, including detecting sarcasm, handling domain-specific language, and ensuring ethical use. Researchers continue to explore new methodologies, datasets, and multimodal inputs (e.g., combining text with images or audio) to enhance accuracy and robustness. Based on different levels of sentiment analysis, it can be categorized into coarse grained document-level sentiment analysis, sentence-level sentiment analysis, and fine-grained aspect-level sentiment analysis. Fine-grained text sentiment analysis is specifically designed to assess objects and their attributes. Fine-grained sentiment analysis, also known as aspect-based sentiment analysis, involves analyzing the sentiment expressed towards specific aspects or entities within a piece of text. Unlike coarse-grained sentiment analysis, which focuses on the overall sentiment of the document, fine-grained sentiment analysis aims to identify and understand the sentiment associated with different aspects, features, or entities mentioned in the text.

2.2 Document-Level SA

This approach analyzes the overall emotional tone of an entire document, classifying it as either positive or negative. The goal is to capture the prevailing sentiment expressed throughout the document, assuming a unified emotional perspective.

2.3 Sentence-Level SA

Moving to a finer grain, sentence-level sentiment analysis examines the emotional or opinionated content within individual sentences, typically classifying them as positive, negative, or neutral. This level presents more complexity due to the concise nature of sentences and the limited number of words expressing emotion. To accurately analyze sentence-level sentiment, it's crucial to distinguish between objective factual statements and subjective expressions of opinion.

2.4 Aspect-Level SA

Aspect-Based Sentiment Analysis (ABSA) has emerged as a pivotal subfield within sentiment analysis, enabling the identification of sentiments tied to specific aspects or attributes of entities. Unlike traditional sentiment classification, which operates at the document or sentence level, ABSA provides a more granular understanding of opinionated content. Recent advancements in attention mechanisms have significantly enhanced the precision and interpretability of ABSA models. Unlike coarse-grained sentiment analysis that assumes a singular emotion, aspect-level sentiment analysis acknowledges that a text can contain multiple viewpoints. For example, a statement like "This phone has an excellent camera and a beautiful design, but its battery life is not strong, and the cost-effectiveness is low" presents both positive and negative sentiments regarding different aspects (camera, design, battery life, cost-effectiveness). Aspect-level analysis focuses on identifying and determining the sentiment polarity for each specific aspect mentioned within a passage, making it possible to capture the nuanced emotional landscape of complex texts.

2.5 Emerging Techniques in Sentiment Analysis

Recent advancements in sentiment analysis have introduced a range of sophisticated techniques that significantly enhance the accuracy and contextual understanding of emotional expressions in text. Among the most notable developments are transformer-based models such as BERT, RoBERTa, and XLNet, which leverage self-attention mechanisms to capture nuanced linguistic patterns and long-range dependencies [3,4]. These models outperform traditional machine learning approaches by offering deeper semantic representation and adaptability across domains. Additionally, multimodal sentiment analysis has gained traction, integrating textual data with complementary modalities such as images, audio to enrich emotional inference. Techniques like cross-modal attention, co-attention networks, and tensor fusion enable more robust sentiment detection by aligning sentiment cues across different data types. Furthermore, self-supervised learning and transfer learning are emerging as powerful strategies to overcome data scarcity and domain-specific limitations, allowing models to generalize better with minimal labeled data. These innovations collectively mark a shift toward more holistic and context-aware sentiment analysis systems, with promising applications in real-time monitoring, customer experience optimization, and social media intelligence [1,2].

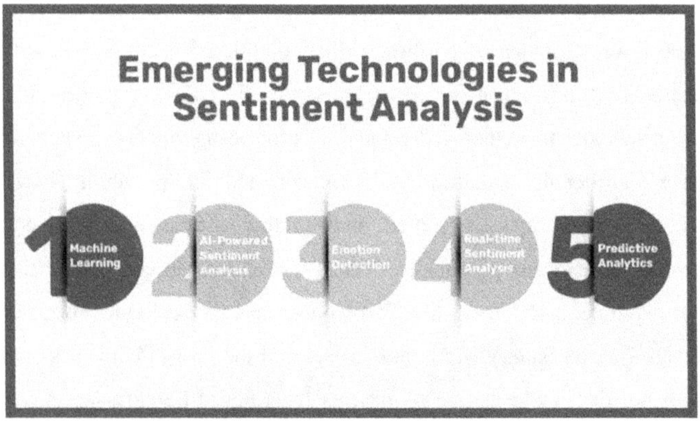

Figure 2.1: Emerging Techniques

Transformer models have revolutionized sentiment analysis by introducing self-attention mechanisms that capture long-range dependencies and contextual relationships in text. Models such as **BERT**, **RoBERTa**, **XLNet**, and **T5** have demonstrated superior performance across various sentiment classification tasks. These models are pre-trained on massive corpora and fine-tuned for specific tasks, enabling them to understand nuanced expressions and domain-specific sentiment cues. For instance, T5 has shown consistent generalization across multiple datasets, while XLNet excels in detecting irony and product-related sentiments. Comparative studies reveal that while BERT offers high accuracy, it demands significant computational resources, whereas GPT models provide faster training with slightly lower precision. Multimodal sentiment analysis (MSA) integrates textual data with other modalities such as images, audio to capture richer emotional signals. This approach is particularly effective in social media contexts, where users express opinions through a blend of text and visuals. Techniques like cross-modal attention, tensor fusion, and hierarchical fusion allow models to align and synthesize sentiment cues across modalities. Recent surveys highlight the growing use of deep learning architectures for multimodal feature extraction and fusion, emphasizing their role in improving sentiment prediction accuracy and robustness4. Despite its promise, MSA faces challenges such as data integration complexity and the scarcity of annotated multimodal datasets. Aspect- Based Sentiment Analysis (ABSA) has evolved to incorporate attention mechanisms that selectively focus on sentiment-bearing words relevant to specific aspects. Models such as BiLSTM with aspect-guided attention, transformer-based cross-attention, and graph attention networks (GATs) enhance aspect–opinion alignment. A recent framework, AdaptiSent, introduced adaptive cross-modal attention to improve aspect term extraction and sentiment classification in multimodal settings, outperforming traditional baselines. These attention-based models are particularly effective in handling complex sentences with multiple aspects and sentiments.

Overview of Sentiment Analysis

2.6 Lexicon-Based Approach

This approach relies on predefined dictionaries or lexicons of sentiment-bearing words.

2.6.1 Dictionary-Based Approach

Uses general sentiment lexicons (e.g., SentiWordNet) to assign polarity scores to words. It assumes that the sentiment of a sentence can be inferred from the sum or average of its word-level sentiments.

2.6.2 Corpus-Based Approach

Builds sentiment lexicons from domain- specific corpora using statistical methods. It often involves identifying co-occurrence patterns between words and known sentiment indicators.

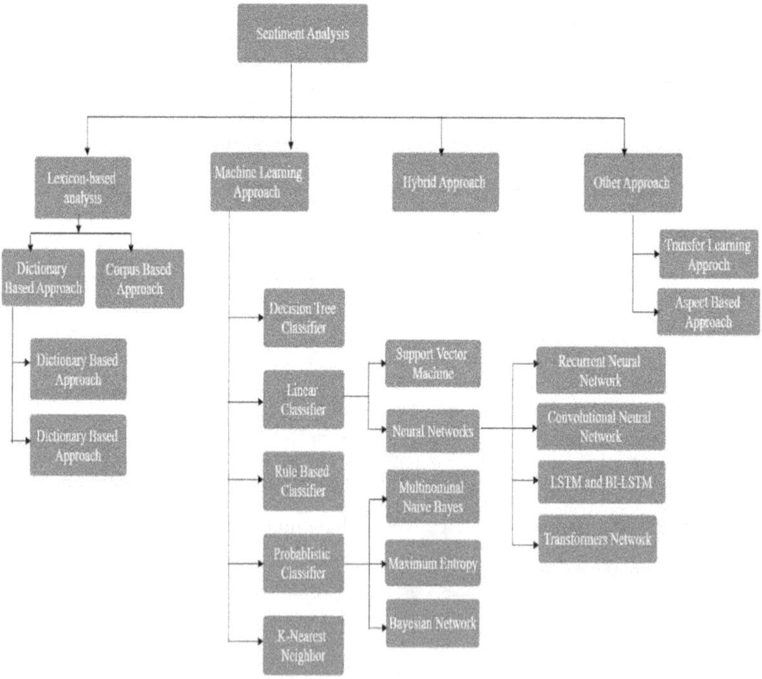

Figure 2.2: Sentiment Classification Techniques

2.7 Machine Learning Approach

This method uses labeled data to train models that can classify sentiment.

- Decision Tree Classifier: Splits data based on feature thresholds to predict sentiment labels.
- Linear Classifier: Includes models like Logistic Regression that use linear decision boundaries.
- Rule-Based Classifier: Applies manually crafted rules to determine sentiment, often used in hybrid systems.
- Probabilistic Classifier: Models like Naive Bayes estimate the probability of sentiment classes given features.
- K-Nearest Neighbor (KNN): Classifies sentiment based on the majority label of the closest data points.[23]

2.8 Hybrid Approach

Combines lexicon-based and machine learning techniques for improved performance.

i. Support Vector Machine (SVM): A powerful classifier that finds the optimal boundary between sentiment classes.

ii. Neural Networks: Includes feed forward and deep neural networks that learn complex patterns.

iii. Multinomial Naive Bayes: A probabilistic model suited for text classification with word frequency features.

iv. Maximum Entropy: A flexible probabilistic model that doesn't assume feature independence.

v. Bayesian Network: Uses probabilistic graphical models to represent dependencies among features.

2.9 Other Approaches

These represent advanced and emerging techniques in sentiment analysis.

i. Transfer Learning Approach: Uses pre-trained models (e.g., BERT, GPT) and fine-tunes them for sentiment tasks. Highly effective in low- resource settings.

ii. Aspect-Based Approach: Focuses on identifying sentiment toward specific aspects or features within text.

a. Recurrent Neural Network (RNN): Captures sequential dependencies in text.

b. Convolutional Neural Network (CNN): Detects local patterns and sentiment phrases.

c. LSTM and Bi-LSTM: Handles long-term dependencies and bidirectional context.

d. Transformers Network: Uses self-attention to model complex relationships and context (e.g., BERT, RoBERTa).

2.10 Aspect Based Sentiment Analysis

ABSA builds on traditional Sentiment Analysis (SA), which classifies text as positive, negative, or neutral.SA treats text holistically, while ABSA dissects it into aspects (e.g., "battery life" or "customer service") and assigns sentiment to each. Aspect Extraction Theory Based on Natural Language Processing (NLP) and Information Extraction, this theory focuses on identifying relevant aspects from text. Compared with the way of off-line shopping in physical stores, users can shop at anytime and anywhere, and do not have to wait for the weekend to go shopping, which saves time and effort. Online shopping offers convenience to consumers, but e- commerce platforms' virtual nature has led to various issues with the products sold on these platforms. These issues include discrepancies between the descriptive information and the actual goods, inferior quality of products and inadequacy of after- sales services [56]. By analyzing consumer sentiment tendencies in their evaluations, it is possible to provide references for other consumers and help e-commerce businesses enhance their service quality and increase consumer satisfaction.

2.10.1 Aspect-Sentiment Pairing

This involves semantic association between aspects and sentiment expressions. Theories here draw from semantic role labeling, co-reference resolution, and attention mechanisms in neural networks. The review on existing works related to multimodal sentimental analysis are discussed below, which focuses on methods they used, the characteristics and their analyzed results. Dependency Parsing: Uses grammatical structure to connect aspect terms with nearby opinion words. Attention Mechanisms: Models like BERT or BiLSTM with attention focus on sentiment-bearing words relevant to each aspect. Aspect Sentiment Triplet Extraction (ASTE): A more advanced task that extracts (aspect, opinion, sentiment) triplets from text. Recent models use contrastive learning to improve pairing accuracy in complex sentences. Unified Generation Models: Sequence-to-sequence models generate aspect– sentiment pairs directly, often using templates or prompts.

Example:
"The ambiance was cozy, but the food was bland."

Aspect–Sentiment Pairs:
Ambiance → Positive Food → Negative

In 2024, Yu Weng *et al.,* [18] introduced a new method called MIECF to improve Multimodal Aspect-based Sentiment Analysis. This approach captures both detailed and overall visual information in an image, integrating key features from numerous perspectives. Local elements, like text and facial expressions, deliver clear emotional signals, while global features contribute to the overall mood and context. To enhance accuracy, the Cross-mixture Fusion technique links these local and global features, reducing confusion and leading to a deeper, more precise sentiment analysis.

In 2024, Licai Sun *et al.,* [19] proposed EMT-DLFR, a unified framework for multimodal learning. By utilizing utterance-level representations as a global context, EMT enabled interaction with local unimodal characteristics, improving both while bypassing the quadratic computational cost of prior local-local cross- modal techniques. To strengthen robustness in incomplete modality scenarios, DLFR reconstructed low-level features, ensuring the model could still learn from missing data. Also, experiments on three benchmark datasets confirm EMT- DLFR's superior performance in both settings.

In 2024, Huiru Wang *et al.,* [20] proposed a multimodal sentiment analysis model based on supervised contrastive learning for richer and more effective data representation. The proposed MLFC module, combining a CNN and Transformer, addresses feature redundancy and filters out irrelevant information. Additionally, supervised contrastive learning enhanced the model's capability to capture sentiment features. Moreover, the evaluations on MVSA-multiple, MVSA-single, and HFM datasets show superior performance over traditional models.

In 2024, Dhendra Marutho *et al.,* [21] introduced a new method that moves from word to sentence embedding using the SBERT transformer model. They improved topic modeling as well as label creation by combining BSC with IDF scoring, allowing better topic identification. The study also integrated the BigBird strategy to improve classification performance.

In 2024, Makera Moayad Aziz *et al.,* [22] developed a new ABSA approach that combines syntax and semantics. Their method, SSDP, uses CoreNLP's dependency parsing and POS tagging to detect sentiment-related patterns effectively. The model captured 75% of sentiment relations, while the remaining data was classified using an LSTM model based on semantic features. Results show that SSDP outperforms other ABSA models that rely only on syntax without advanced data processing. The study also points out the weaknesses of such models and suggests improvements through better data handling.

In 2025, Stefan Lam *et al.,* [23] developed SS-LIME and SS-LORE, leveraging the Anchor framework to interpret two cutting-edge ABSA deep learning models. These models are extensions of the LCR-Rot architecture, with LCR-Rot-hop incorporating multiple iterations of the attention rotatory mechanism and LCR-Rot- hop++ further integrating context-dependent word embeddings and hierarchical attention. The study finds that LCR-Rot-hop++ offers superior interpretability compared to LCR-Rot-hop.

In 2024, Kamran Aziz *et al.,* [24] introduced an improved version of UrduAspectNet, designed for ABSA in Urdu. The model enhances accuracy by integrating BiLSTM, dual GCNs and Biaffine Attention with XLM-R embeddings. Moreover, the dependence parsing helps to construct an adjacency matrix, allowing the GCNs to capture syntactic relationships effectively. Named Enhanced UrduAspectNet, this version also incorporated lemma embeddings and POS, processed via GCN and BiLSTM layers, with Biaffine Attention refining aspect-sentiment extraction.

In 2023, Jingli Shi *et al.,* [25] introduced a unified framework for aspect-based sentiment analysis, integrating a graph convolutional network with multi-layer semantic and syntax modules. Semantic features enhance syntactic learning, while two attention mechanisms refine dependency relations and aspect-opinion term boundaries. Experiments on four datasets confirm its superiority over existing models.

In 2022, Meng Xu, *et al.,* [26] proposed a novel multimodal sentiment analysis framework called CMJRT, which captures hierarchical interactions between modalities by transferring joint representations from bimodal to unimodal settings. Using cyclic translation, one modality was forward and backward translated into the other through encoder-decoders, ensuring consistency between them. Additionally, a cross-modal transformer was employed to strengthen every unimodal representation with shared evidence from bimodality, enhancing complementarity.

In 2023, Yuxia Zhao, *et al.,* [27] presented a multimodal sentiment analysis method that leveraged multiple emotional information sources to aid decision-making. The CRNN-SVM model was identified as the most effective for sentiment tendency recognition in DL, making it ideal for sentiment analysis system design. The main contribution of this work was overcoming the limitations of single-mode emotion assessment by introducing a multimodal scheme, incorporated CNN to provide better meet user needs and more emotional insights.

Table 2.1 pinpoints benefits and disadvantages on extant studies using various methodologies are tabulated.

Table 2.1: Features and challenges on existing works

Sr.No.	**Authors [citation]**	**Methods**	**Benefits**	**Disadvantages**
1	Yu Weng *et al.,*[18]	MICEF	Achieved balanced and cohesive visual data extraction to reduce modality gaps.	Need to explore the method's applicability in different domains to gauge its versatility.

2	Licai Sun *et al.,*[19]	EMT-DLFR	The technique increased sentence length while preserving label integrity.	Still it faces quadratic complexity relative to input length.
3	Huiru Wang *et al.,*[20]	CNN	Suppress irrelevant data to focus on meaningful features.	Necessary to mitigate the problem of redundant feature information.
4	Dhendra Marutho *et al.,* [21]	SBERT transformer model	Identified the optimal cluster through adaptive Bayesian Search, resulting in 45 candidate labels.	Need for more optimization to make the method universally applicable to various review categories beyond hotel reviews.
5	Makera Moayad Aziz *et al.,* [22]	SSDP Method with CoreNLP, and LSTM	Examined the relationship between opinion targets and sentiment words for contextual understanding.	Additional studies were needed to investigate failure cases and refine the model for complex situations.
6	Stefan Lam *et al.,*[23]	SS-LORE and SS-LIME	Adapted SP algorithm into the WSP algorithm, prioritizing instances containing opinionated features.	Ensured balanced neighborhoods in the SS method to improve clarity.
7	Kamran Aziz *et al.,* [24]	Bi-LSTMs and GCNs	Leveraged XLM-R embeddings to strengthen Urdu linguistic processing.	Necessitated Improved preprocessing techniques to better manage informal language variations.
8	Jingli Shi *et al.,*[25]	Unified syntax-enhanced network	Multi-layer attention in MSS enabled the detection of indirect term connections, ensuring precise target extraction.	Required a structured approach to integrating multiple attention mechanisms for indirect connections.

9	Meng Xu, *et al.,*[26]	CMJRT	It obtained low fitting error.	Need to investigate the weighting of modalities through joint representations to achieve further improvements.
10	Yuxia Zhao, *et al.,* [27]	CRNN-SVM	It acquired maximal strength and competent for high load long term operation.	Need to consider the limitations of sample.

Table 2.2: Imminent Research Done to Identify Human Sentiments in Medical Field

Sr.No.	Title	Algorithm/ Technique	Data set/ source	Language used for Data set
1	Long Short Term Memory based Sentiment Analysis of Healthcare	LSTM algorithm	Healthcare review data	English
2	Deep Learning Based sentiment Analysis on Drug Reviews	Deep learning and machine learning Techniques LSTM and BiLSTM	Medicine reviews from web	English
3	Exploring Drug sentiment Analysis with Machine Learnings Techniques.	Machine learning algorithms	Publicly available dataset of drug reviews	English
4	Hybrid CNN LBP using Facial emotion Recognition based on deep learning approach	The Convolutional Neural Network (CNN) algorithm	Not specify	English
5	LSTM Based Sentiment Analysis Conversant ions in Health	LSTM with Deep Learning	healthcare existing data	English

In Long Short Term Memory-based Sentiment Analysis of Healthcare Reviews, the authors employ an LSTM algorithm to model sequential dependencies in language and classify sentiments over healthcare review data, highlighting the suitability of recurrent architectures for domain-specific patient narratives. Deep Learning Based Sentiment Analysis on Drug Reviews extends this idea by comparing deep learning and traditional machine learning—with LSTM and BiLSTM prominently featured—on medicine reviews scraped from the web, showing the benefits of bidirectional context for polarity detection. Exploring Drug Sentiment Analysis with Machine Learning Techniques focuses on conventional classifiers applied to a publicly available dataset of drug reviews, providing a baseline perspective on feature engineering versus learned representations. Hybrid CNN LBP using Facial Emotion Recognition based on Deep Learning Approach pivots to visual affect, using a Convolutional Neural Network augmented with Local Binary Patterns for facial emotion recognition, though the dataset is not specified, which limits reproducibility and direct comparability to text-based studies. Finally, LSTM Based Sentiment Analysis Conversations in Health applies deep learning with LSTM to existing healthcare conversational data, underscoring the model's capacity to capture context in dialogue while reinforcing the trend toward recurrent and deep architectures in health-related sentiment analysis.

Sentiment analysis is the detection of attitudes, "enduring, affectively colored beliefs, and dispositions towards objects or persons". We have to consider following important factors:

1. Holder (source) of attitude
2. Target (aspect) of attitude
3. Type of attitude
   - From a set of types
   - Like, love, hate, value, desire, etc.
   - Or (more commonly) simple weighted polarity
   - positive, negative, neutral, together with strength
4. Text containing the attitude
   - Sentence or the entire document

Affective states refer to the emotional states or moods that individual's experience, and they play a crucial role in sentiment analysis. Sentiment analysis involves determining the sentiment or emotional tone expressed in a piece of text, and affective states contribute to this understanding. Here are some key affective states often considered in sentiment analysis are:

1) Emotion: It is a brief organically synchronized and evaluation of a major event e.g. angry, sad, joyful, fearful, ashamed, proud, and elated.
2) Mood: It is diffuse non-caused low-intensity long-duration change in subjective feeling e.g. cheerful, gloomy, irritable, listless, and depressed.
3) Interpersonal stances: It is an affective stance toward another person in a specific interaction e.g. friendly, flirtatious, distant, cold, warm, supportive, and contemptuous.
4) Attitudes: It is enduring, affectively colored beliefs, dispositions towards objects or persons e.g. liking, loving, hating, valuing, desiring.
5) Personality traits: stable personality dispositions and typical behavior tendencies examples are nervous, anxious, reckless, morose, hostile, and jealous.

The presence of specific linguistic features, such as intensifiers or sentiment-laden phrases, correlates with the assignment of more extreme sentiment categories (e.g., very positive or very negative) in fine-grained sentiment analysis.

Introducing a fine-grained sentiment analysis model with an aspect-based attention mechanism will significantly improve the accuracy and granularity of sentiment classification by dynamically focusing on different aspects of the text. Aspect- based Attention: The hypothesis assumes that incorporating an aspect-based attention mechanism will allow the model to selectively attend to different aspects or components of the text. By dynamically adjusting attention weights, the model can focus on specific entities, topics, or aspects within the input text, thereby capturing more nuanced sentiment expressions related to each aspect. Improved Granularity: The hypothesis suggests that fine-grained sentiment analysis, enabled by aspect-based attention, will lead to improved granularity in sentiment classification. Instead of assigning a single sentiment label to the entire text, the model can identify and analyze sentiments at a more granular level, considering various aspects independently. This granularity can provide richer insights into the nuanced sentiments expressed within the text.

Aspect-Specific Sentiment

Representation: By leveraging aspect-based attention, the hypothesis proposes that the model will be able to generate aspect-specific representations of sentiment within the text. This means that the sentiment expressed towards different aspects or entities within the text can be captured separately, allowing for more precise sentiment analysis. Hypothesis posits that incorporating an aspect-based attention mechanism into fine-grained sentiment analysis models will lead to more accurate, granular, and adaptable sentiment classification, thereby improving the performance and utility of sentiment analysis applications across various domains and use cases.

2.11 Identified Research Gaps

Despite significant advancements in fine-grained sentiment analysis, particularly in aspect-based modeling and attention-driven architectures, several critical gaps remain unaddressed. This chapter outlines the limitations observed in existing literature and identifies areas that warrant further exploration to enhance the precision, adaptability, and interpretability of sentiment analysis systems.

- **Limited Domain and Dataset Diversity**

  Most existing ABSA models are trained on narrowly scoped datasets such as restaurant or product reviews. This domain specificity restricts the generalizability of models to broader contexts like healthcare, education, or finance. Moreover, the scarcity of annotated datasets across diverse domains and languages poses a challenge for robust model development.

- **Underutilization of Multimodal Data**

  Current fine-grained sentiment analysis frameworks predominantly rely on textual data, overlooking the rich emotional cues embedded in audio and visual modalities. The lack of effective multimodal fusion strategies and alignment mechanisms limits the depth of sentiment interpretation, especially in real-world applications.

- **Aspect Ambiguity and Overlapping Sentiments**

  Sentences often contain multiple aspects with varying sentiment polarities, leading to ambiguity in aspect identification and classification. Existing models struggle to disambiguate nested or overlapping aspect-opinion pairs, which affects the granularity and accuracy of sentiment predictions.

- **Lack of Explainability in Deep Models**

  While attention mechanisms enhance performance, they often lack transparency. Most models do not provide interpretable outputs that justify sentiment predictions, making it difficult for users to understand the rationale behind classification decisions. This limits trust and usability in sensitive domains.

- **Cross-Lingual and Low-Resource Limitations**

  ABSA research is heavily skewed toward English-language datasets, with minimal support for low-resource languages. Cross-lingual transfer learning and multilingual sentiment modeling remain underexplored, hindering the global applicability of current approaches.

- **Absence of Temporal and Contextual Modeling**

  Sentiment is dynamic and context-dependent, often influenced by temporal shifts, sarcasm, or negation. Few models incorporate temporal tracking or context-aware attention mechanisms, resulting in static interpretations that fail to capture evolving emotional states.

Inadequate Evaluation Frameworks

Standard metrics such as accuracy and F1-score may not fully capture the complexity of fine-grained sentiment analysis. There is a need for task-specific evaluation protocols that assess aspect-level precision, sentiment intensity, and interpretability.

Table 2.3: Mental Health Problems Associated with Emotions

Negative Emotion	Associated Mental Health Problems	Notes
 Anxiety	Generalized Anxiety Disorder (GAD), Panic Disorder	Chronic worry, restlessness, physical symptoms like rapid heartbeat
 Sadness	Major Depressive Disorder, Dysthymia	Persistent low mood, loss of interest, fatigue
 Anger	Intermittent Explosive Disorder, Conduct Disorder	Aggression, irritability, difficulty managing impulses
 Fear	Phobias, PTSD, Panic Disorder	Avoidance behaviors, flashbacks, hypervigilance
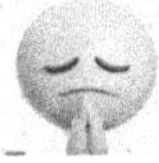 Guilt	Depression, OCD	Rumination, self-blame, compulsive behaviors
 Shame	Social Anxiety Disorder, Depression	Withdrawal, low self-esteem, self-criticism
 Disappointment	Adjustment Disorders, Depression	Difficulty coping with unmet expectations
 Jealousy/Insecurity	Borderline Personality Disorder, Anxiety	Emotional instability, fear of abandonment
 Loneliness	Depression, Substance Use Disorders	Isolation, lack of social support, increased risk of addiction

2.12 Summary

The gaps identified above highlight the need for more inclusive, interpretable, and context-aware sentiment analysis models. Addressing these challenges will require the development of domain-adaptive architectures, multimodal fusion techniques, explainable AI frameworks, and multilingual datasets. These directions form the foundation for the subsequent chapters, which propose a novel hybrid framework to overcome these limitations. Aspect-Based Sentiment Analysis (ABSA) using multimodal data is an advanced approach to understanding user opinions by analyzing both textual and visual inputs. Unlike traditional sentiment analysis, which assigns a general sentiment to an entire piece of content, ABSA focuses on specific aspects—such as "battery life" or "design"—and determines the sentiment expressed toward each one. When multimodal data is involved, models integrate textual cues with visual features (like product images or social media photos) to enhance accuracy and contextual understanding. Recent innovations include dual syntactic graph networks that capture complex linguistic structures, contrastive learning techniques that align image and text representations and cross-attention mechanisms that allow deeper interaction between modalities [66]. Large Language Models (LLMs) are also being used to generate rationales that guide smaller models in making more informed predictions. Evaluated on datasets like TWITTER-2015 and TWITTER-2017, these systems show improved performance in aspect-level sentiment classification. As research progresses, multimodal ABSA is expected to expand into video and audio domains, offering richer insights for applications in e-commerce, social media monitoring, and personalized recommendations The reviewed literature highlights a progressive evolution in sentiment analysis techniques, particularly within healthcare and drug-related domains. Early studies such as Long Short Term Memory-based Sentiment Analysis of Healthcare Reviews *and* LSTM Based Sentiment Analysis Conversations *in Health* demonstrate the effectiveness of LSTM architectures in capturing sequential patterns and emotional tone in patient narratives. Building on this, *Deep Learning Based Sentiment Analysis on Drug Reviews* incorporates both LSTM and BiLSTM models to enhance polarity detection in medicine-related texts, showcasing the advantages of bidirectional context modeling. In contrast, Exploring Drug Sentiment

Analysis with Machine Learning Techniques adopts traditional machine learning algorithms on publicly available drug review datasets, offering baseline comparisons and emphasizing the role of feature engineering.. They also reveal a research gap in integrating multimodal data and aspect-level granularity, which this thesis aims to address through an attention-drive [8].

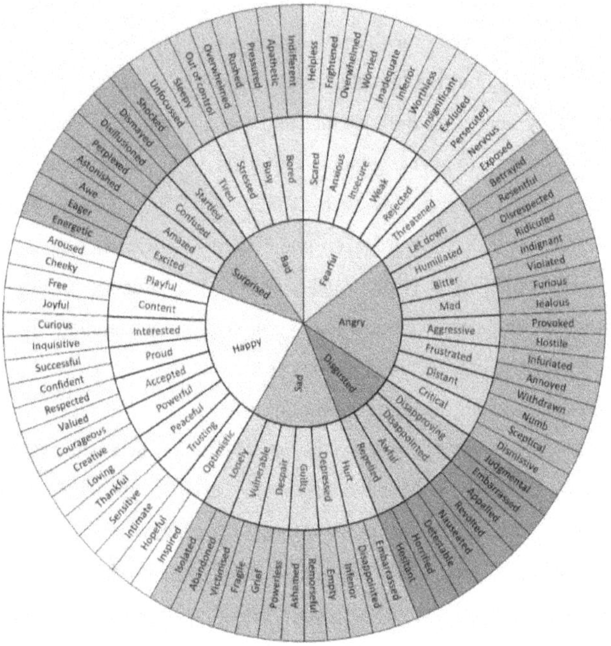

Figure 2.3: Shades of Positive and Negative Emotions

In sentiment analysis, emotions are rarely expressed in binary extremes; instead, they manifest in varying shades of positivity and negativity. These subtle gradations—ranging from mild satisfaction to intense joy or from slight irritation to profound anger—play a critical role in accurately interpreting sentiment. Capturing these emotional nuances allows models to move beyond simplistic polarity classification and toward more refined sentiment scoring. For instance, phrases like "somewhat pleased" or "deeply disappointed" convey different intensities that influence aspect-level sentiment weighting. In multimodal sentiment analysis, these shades are further enriched by vocal tone, facial expression, and contextual cues, making it essential to design models that can detect and quantify emotional depth across modalities. By incorporating these variations, sentiment analysis systems become more sensitive to human affect, enabling more precise and context-aware predictions [52-80].

Multiclass sentiment analysis is an advanced approach in natural language processing that aims to classify textual data into more than two sentiment categories, such as "positive," "negative," "neutral," and additional nuanced emotions like "anger," "joy," "sadness," or "sarcasm." Unlike binary sentiment analysis, which offers limited insight, multiclass classification enables a deeper understanding of user opinions and emotional tone. This method typically involves sophisticated preprocessing steps including tokenization, stop word removal, lemmatization, and handling of negations, followed by feature extraction using techniques like TF-IDF, Word2Vec, or contextual embeddings such as BERT. Machine learning algorithms like Support Vector Machines (SVM), Random Forests, and Naive Bayes, as well as deep learning models like LSTM and transformers, are commonly employed to handle the complexity of multiple sentiment classes. Recent studies have demonstrated that integrating linguistic features, dependency parsing, and hierarchical classification structures can significantly improve performance in multiclass sentiment tasks. This approach is particularly valuable in domains such as social media monitoring, customer feedback analysis, and opinion mining, where understanding the full spectrum of sentiment is crucial for actionable insights [81-92].

CHAPTER 3
RESEARCH METHODOLOGY

Research methodology refers to the structured framework and systematic approach that researchers use to conduct a study. It encompasses the tools, techniques, and procedures applied to collect, analyze, and interpret data in order to answer research questions or test hypotheses. Essentially, it's the blueprint of how research is carried out—from the philosophical foundations and research design to the methods of data collection and analysis.

A well-defined research methodology ensures that the study is reliable, valid, and replicable. It helps researchers stay focused, make informed decisions, and produce credible results. Depending on the nature of the study, methodologies can be **quantitative** (focused on numerical data), **qualitative** (focused on descriptive data), or **mixed-methods** (a combination of both). Choosing the right methodology is crucial because it directly influences the accuracy and depth of the findings.

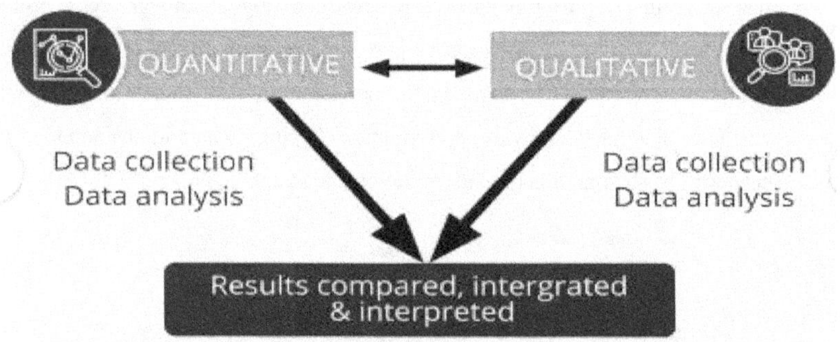

Figure 3.1: Research Method

3.1 Research Framework

Multimodal Sentiment Analysis (MSA) is a cutting-edge approach in sentiment analysis that leverages multiple data modalities such as text, audio, and image, to more accurately interpret human emotions and opinions. Traditional sentiment analysis primarily focuses on textual data, but human communication is inherently multimodal, involving speech tone, facial expressions, and body language, which provide deeper emotional context. By integrating these diverse data sources, multimodal sentiment analysis enhances the accuracy and robustness of emotion detection, making it highly valuable in applications. Hence, this paper proposes a novel Position Attention Module assisted LeNet-based Multimodal Sentiment Analysis (PAM-LNet-MSA) framework. The architecture of proposed PAM-LNet-MSA is shown in Figure 3.2.

In a PAM-LNet-MSA system, the process begins with the input phase, where three types of data such as text, image, and audio are fed into the system. Each modality undergoes a distinct preprocessing step to prepare the data for further examination. For text, the process includes tokenization that breaks the text into smaller units such as words or phrases, followed by stemming to diminish words to their base-root form, helping in uniformity. The input images are processed using a Gaussian filter that smooths the image to reduce noise, while audio undergoes low-pass filtering to remove high-frequency noise, retaining only the relevant low-frequency components [27]. A Gaussian filter is employed when the task is primarily noise reduction and smoothing of static data (like images), because it is simple, efficient, and does not require a model of the Complex system. In contrast, the Kalman filter is designed for dynamic systems where recursive state estimation is needed. Thus, Gaussian filters are chosen in contexts like image preprocessing, while Kalman filters are used in tracking or time-series estimation. Gaussian filter uses the domain image processing, static signals where as Kalman filter use in the domain like robotics ,navigation ,time series .

This hybrid multimodal sentiment analysis model integrates image, audio, and text inputs to enhance sentiment classification accuracy. Each modality undergoes specialized preprocessing and feature extraction—PHOG and LGIP for visual cues, spectral and EMD techniques for audio signals, and DL-ATE for aspect-based text features. These diverse features are fused using S-MIFF to retain maximum informative value, and then passed through a hybrid classifier combining PAM-LNet and SqueezeNet. The model outputs sentiment across three classes, demonstrating a robust and comprehensive approach to capturing nuanced emotional expressions across next, the system moves to feature extraction. For text, Deep Learning-based Aspect Term Extraction (DL-ATE) is performed to identify the definite entities or topics within the text that are relevant for sentiment analysis. Additionally, TF-IDF is used to calculate the significance of words in a document related to the entire dataset. For images, PHOG is used to capture the spatial structure of the image, while LGIP extracts texture features by analyzing local image patches. In the audio domain, EMD decomposes the audio signal into intrinsic mode functions, and spectral features are extracted to capture frequency components of the sound.

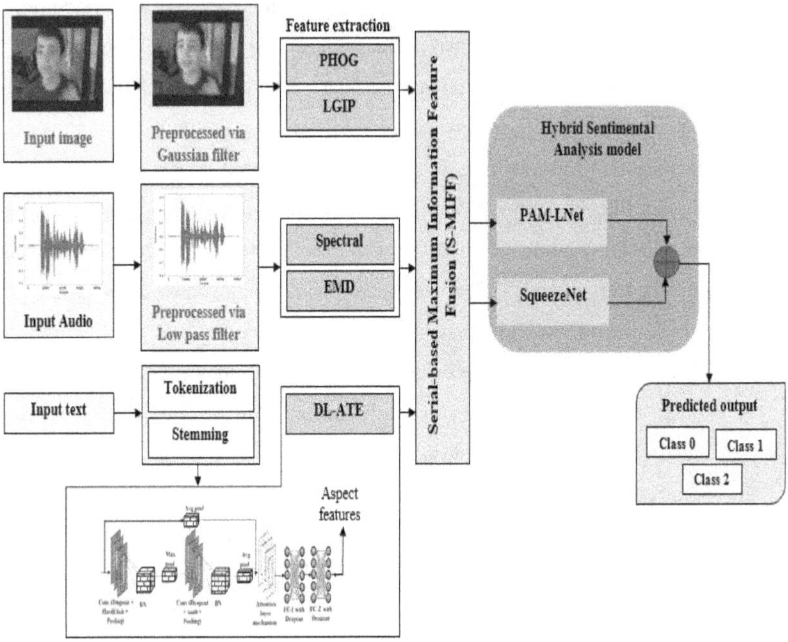

Figure 3.2: Overview of PAM-SNet-MSA

After feature extraction, the feature fusion phase integrates the features from all three modalities using a Serial-based Maximum Information Feature Fusion (S-MIFF) approach, where features from text, image, and audio are combined in a sequential manner. This unified feature set is then passed through a Hybrid sentiment analysis model, where advanced convolutional neural networks like

Position Attention Module assisted LeNet (PAM-LNet) and SqueezeNet are applied. These models are specifically designed to progress the precision of sentiment prediction by leveraging the deep hierarchical characteristics from the multimodal data. Finally, the system outputs the final analyzed result, which provides a comprehensive sentiment evaluation based on the combined understanding of text, audio, and image data, offering more accurate and nuanced insights compared to single-modality analysis.

3.2 Preprocessing

The preprocessing stage in fine-grained sentiment analysis is crucial for transforming raw textual data into a structured format suitable for model training. It begins with collecting raw text input, which may come from sources like reviews, social media posts, or customer feedback. This text is then cleaned to remove noise such as HTML tags, emojis, punctuation, and unnecessary whitespace. Next, all text is converted to lowercase to ensure uniformity and reduce redundancy. Tokenization follows, where the text is split into individual words or sub-words, allowing for granular analysis. Common stop-words—words that do not contribute meaningful sentiment, like "the" or "is"—are removed to focus on more informative terms. Lemmatization or stemming is applied to reduce words to their base forms, helping unify variations like "running" and "ran." Handling negations is a critical step, as phrases like "not good" carry different sentiment than "good," and must be treated accordingly.

After this, sentiment labels are mapped to each text sample, typically ranging from very positive to very negative, enabling fine-grained classification. The cleaned and labeled text is then vectorized using techniques like TF-IDF, Word2Vec, or BERT embeddings to convert it into numerical format. Finally, the dataset is split into training and testing sets—often using stratified sampling to preserve label distribution—so that the model can be trained and evaluated effectively. This structured pipeline ensures that the data fed into the sentiment analysis model is clean, consistent, and rich in sentiment-relevant features. Preprocessing plays a vital role in multimodal sentiment analysis pipeline. In order to ensures uniformity across data from different sources (text, image, audio), making it easier to integrate and analyze. Let assume I^{Txt}, I^{Img}, and I^{Aud} be the input text, image and audio, respectively. As each modality has distinct features, the preprocessing steps for each modality are discussed as follows:

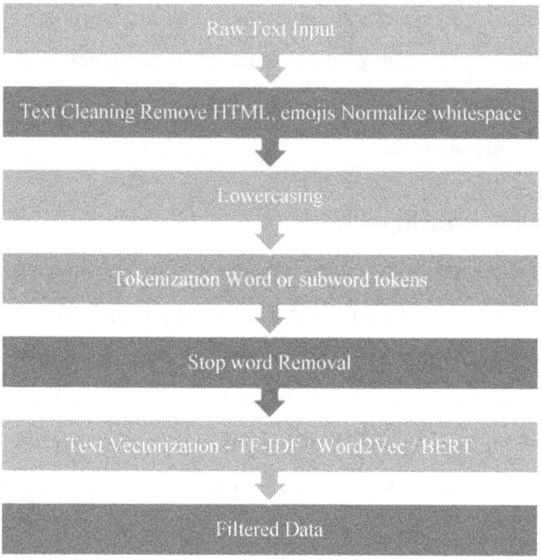

Figure 3.3: Preprocessing for fine Grain Sentiment Analysis

3.3 Text preprocessing

Text 1st typically contains noise, irrelevant words, and inconsistencies. The data Pre-processing for text aims to clean and standardize the data for further investigation.

The common steps involved are as follows:

Tokenization: Tokenization [28] is the process of dividing a sentence into distinct tokens, such as words or symbols, and is achieved through the split () method. For example, the sentence-"The movie was absolutely amazing with great performances and a compelling storyline" will be splitted into tokens as 'The', 'movie', 'was', 'absolutely', 'amazing', 'with', 'great', 'performances', 'and', 'a', 'compelling', and 'storyline'. This output is fed into the further stemming process.

Stemming: Stemming is a technique employed in pre-processing to strip suffixes from words, find their base form, reduce the word count, and save both memory and time. The stemming process is applied to the above tokens and obtain the stemmed output as 'The', 'movie', 'was', 'absolute', 'amaze', 'with', 'great', 'performance', 'and', 'a', 'compel', and 'storyline'.Thus, the preprocessed text is denoted as I^{Txt}.

3.4 Image preprocessing

Images I^{img} need to be processed to eliminate noise, adjust brightness/ contrast, and Enhance important features before feature extraction. In this work, the input image, I^{img} is preprocessed using Gaussian filtering technique.

Gaussian filtering: Gaussian filtering [29] is a technique, which is used to reduce noise and smooth images or signals. It works by applying a Gaussian function to I^{img} where each point in I^{img} *is* weighted based on its distance from the center. The two dimensional Gaussian filtering is formulated as in Eq. (1). Here, σ 2 refers to variance.

$$Gaus(p,q) = \frac{1}{2\pi\sigma^2} e^{-\left(p^2+q^2\right)/2\sigma^2} \tag{1}$$

Thus, the preprocessed image is denoted by ${}_{Pre}I^{img}$

3.5 Audio preprocessing

Audio I^{Aud} and is highly susceptible to noise and inconsistencies. Preprocessing helps to data clean I^{Aud} and extract the relevant features for sentiment analysis using the low pass filtering approach.

Low-pass filtering: A low-pass filter permits signals below the cut-off frequency to pass, while filtering out higher frequencies. Ideally, this filter would perfectly transmit frequencies within the pass band, fully attenuate frequencies in the stop band, and exhibit a sharp transition between the two to minimize any loss of data. Among various low pass filtering technique, this work adopts Butterworth filter [30] approach to preprocess I^{Aud}.

The Butterworth filter is a frequency-based filter that improves the signal spectra according to a specified cut-off frequency. In the frequency domain, the magnitude response of Butterworth filter is expressed as in Eq. (2).

$$\left|B\left(kI_{\omega}^{Aud}\right)\right| = \frac{1}{\sqrt{1+\left(\frac{I_{\omega}^{Aud}}{\omega_c}\right)^{2N}}} \tag{2}$$

where, $B\left(kI_{\omega}^{Aud}\right)$ indicates response magnitude; I_{ω}^{Aud} input frequency of I^{Aud}; k refers to imaginary unit; N denotes filter order and ω_c refers to particular cut-off frequency.

Then, the preprocessed audio is denoted as ${}_{Pre}I^{Aud}$.

3.6 Feature extraction

Feature extraction is a crucial step in multimodal sentiment analysis, as it converts preprocessed data from text I^{Txt}, ${}_{Pre}I^{Img}$ and audio ${}_{Pre}I^{Aud}$ into structured features images that deep learnings models can that deep learning model can use for sentiment classifications. This process focuses on identifying the key information within each modality, allowing the model to better understand and interpret the data[33].

3.6.1 Text feature extraction

For the preprocessed text data, ${}_{Pre}I^{Txt}$ the goal is to capture meaningful features that help in sentiment analysis, such as specific terms or concepts that contribute to the sentiment. Common feature extraction methods for text includes are as follows:

DL-ATE: Aspect Term Extraction (ATE) [31] is a key task in Sentiment Analysis that involves identifying specific aspects (or features) of an entity from a given text ${}_{Pre}I^{Txt}$. In order to retrieve the aspect term from ${}_{Pre}I^{Txt}$, this work adopts Deep Learning-based Aspect Term Extraction (DL-ATE). While training time, the computed aspect terms are fed into the Deep Convolutional Neural network with Attention Mechanism (DCNN-AM) [32] model to train it. Conversely, the aspect features are extracted from ${}_{Pre}I^{Txt}$ via DCNN-AM model, while testing time. The concept of DL-ATE process is determined as follows:

Train DCNN-AM using computed Aspect term: The aspect term extractor initi ally conducts token-level classification for each individual token. Let $T_{{}_{Pre}I^{Txt}}$ represent the preprocessed text features ${}_{Pre}I^{Txt}$ associated with the corresponding position of token T. The aspect term extractor is formulated as in Eq. (3).

$$A_{trm} = \frac{\exp\left(T_{{}_{Pre}I^{Txt}}\right)}{\sum_{k=1}^{N} \exp\left(T_{{}_{Pre}I^{Txt}}\right)} \tag{3}$$

DCNN-AM model: DCNN is a deep learning architecture planned for processing structured data. It consists of numerous layers and making them highly effective for sentimental analysis. The main limitation of this is increased layers count between input and output and two set of parameters, in which one set represents the filter coefficients and another set of weights in the FC network need to be leveraged. Such issues could be overcome by using attention layer mechanism, dropout and residual connection.

The proposed DCNN-AM architecture starts with a preprocessed text input, ${}_{Pre}I^{Txt}$ which undergoes multiple transformations through "convolutional layers, pooling layers, batch normalization, and activation functions". As shown in Figure 2, the input ${}_{Pre}I^{Txt}$ passes through a convolutional layer followed by dropout, which helps prevent over-fitting. The activation function used here is HardElish [33], which introduces non-linearity. A pooling layer is then applied to reduce the spatial dimensions, followed by batch normalization (BN) to stabilize learning. Afterward, max pooling further down samples the feature maps.

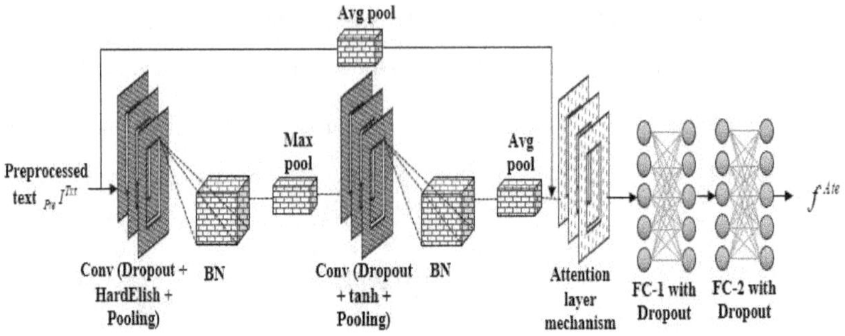

Figure 3.4: DCNN-AM Architecture

Next, another convolutional layer is applied, followed by dropout and the tanh activation function, which helps in capturing both positive and negative feature representations. This is followed by another pooling layer, BN, and average pooling 1, which further refines the features. Simultaneously, the input also undergoes a separate average pooling 2 operation. The outputs from average pooling 1 and 2 are concatenated, combining important contextual information from both pathways. This fused feature representation is then passed through an attention layer, which helps the network focus on the most relevant features. After attention processing, the features pass through two fully connected layers, each followed by dropout with improved loss function, ensuring robust learning and reducing over-fitting.

Traditionally, Dice loss function [34] is used as in Eq. (4). To reduce the computational complexity and faster convergence, inverse combo dice loss is proposed. The inverse combo loss is defined as in Eq. (5). Further, applying dice loss to inverse combo loss is expressed as in Eq. (6).

$$Dl(y,\hat{p}) = \left[1 - \frac{2y\hat{p}+1}{y+\hat{p}+1}\right] \tag{4}$$

$$f(x) = \left[\frac{1}{\sum_{i=1}^{N}(y_i - \hat{p})^2 / N}\right] \tag{5}$$

$$f'(x) = \left[f(x) + \left[\frac{1}{1+e^{-(Dl(y,\hat{p}))}}\right]\right] \tag{6}$$

Thereby, the DCNN-AM model appropriately performed well in the training algorithms to diminish the parameter adjustment count. The need for weight modifications in the FC layer is greatly reduced, enabling better learning in the convolutional layer and enhancing aspect term extraction as f^{Ate}.

TF-IDF: TF-IDF [35], f^{tf-idf} is a metric that determines the relevance of a term T in a document D compared to the whole corpus ς, calculated through Eq. (7).

$$T - Idf_{T,D} = Tf_{T,D} * Idf_T \tag{7}$$

where, $Tf_{T,D} = \frac{No.of\ occu\ of\ T \in D}{Total\ length\ of\ D}$ and $Idf_T = \log_{10}\left(\frac{No.of\ doc \in \varsigma}{No.of\ doc\ of\ \varsigma\ contain\ the\ term\ T}\right)$.

Thus, the proposed approach reduces the parameter adjustments count. The procedure of weight adjustment in FC layer diminished knowingly that focus the learning of convolutional layer.

Thus, the text features extracted from preprocessed text are represented as $ft_1 = \left[f^{Ate}, f^{tf-idf}\right]$.

3.6.2 Image feature extraction

For the preprocessed image $_{Pre}I^{Img}$, the feature extraction process focuses on identifying visual patterns, shapes, textures, and other characteristics that are relevant for sentiment analysis are discussed in the following:

PHOG: Pyramid Histogram of Oriented Gradients [36] represents an image at various resolutions using HOG features and spatial information from local segments. The image is divided into multiple areas at distinct resolutions, and segments are squared along axes to form increasing spatial grids. The sum of points in four cells at each level represents the pyramid structure. Gradient calculations are performed using the Sobel operator, with the gradient and orientation, g^{orient} equations shown in Eq. (8) and Eq. (9).

$$g = \sqrt{g_u^2 + g_v^2} \tag{8}$$

$$g^{orient} = \arctan\left(g_u / g_v \right) \tag{9}$$

The histogram cells are generated with pixel weights according to g^{orient}, using a range of angles. Two matrices are formed: "one with gradient sums and the other with magnitudes". The HOG is computed for the global space, and the image is separated into four spatial areas. The process repeats until a predefined level is reached, integrating HOG features from all regions to construct the final PHOG descriptor f^{phog}, with its length calculated by Eq. (10).

$$Len = bin \times \left(4^0 + 4^1 + ... + 4^{level}\right) \tag{10}$$

LGIP: The LBP feature works by comparing the intensity of each pixel with its 8 neighboring pixels, assigning 8 binary bits, which are then converted into a decimal label, as represented in Eq. (11).

$$lbp(y_c, z_c) = \sum_{x=0}^{7} l(I_x - I_c) \tag{11}$$

where, $l(s) = \begin{cases} 1, & s \geq 0 \\ 0, & s < 0 \end{cases}$; I_c denotes intensity of central pixel; and I_x denotes intensity of xth neighbor.

LGIP [37] captures local intensity trends by calculating gradient responses using eight Sobel masks and assigning an 8-bit code based on the responses. It improves stability against noise and lighting changes, and the Overall Trend Vector (OTV) is computed by summing 1-valued vectors. The OTV is assigned an LGIP code via a 2D lookup table. LGIP outperforms LBP by being faster, more stable against noise, and having lower dimensionality, making it more efficient for image-to-image distance calculations and this provides the LGIP descriptor as f^{lgip}.

Thus, the extracted image features are denoted as $ft_2 = \left[f^{phog}, f^{lgip}\right]$.

3.6.3 Audio feature extraction

Audio data requires specific techniques to capture important features related to tone, pitch, rhythm, and other acoustic characteristics that convey sentiment. Some common feature extraction methods for audio include:

EMD: EMD [38] serves as an efficient method for analyzing non-linear and non-stationary data, frequently applied in speech signal processing. It decomposes a given signal into several oscillatory modes determined as Intrinsic Mode Functions (IMFs) along with a residue, as indicated in Eq. (12).

$$Emd(c) = \sum_{i=1}^{n} H_i(t) + R_n(t) \tag{12}$$

Where, $R_n(t)$ denotes residue and $H_i(t)$ indicates Intrinsic mode function.

Spectral features: The spectral features [39] f^{spec} are calculated using the Short-Time Fourier Transform (STFT) of the signal. Among various metrics, this work uses spectral centroid metrics to extract.

The spectral centroid represents the "center of mass" of a spectrum. It is closely connected to the perceived "brightness" of a sound. This can be evaluated as the weighted mean of frequencies using their magnitudes as weights via Fourier transform, the centroid reflects the spectral shape. The spectral centroid is formulated as in Eq. (13).

$$Cent(\mu) = \int fr.K(fr).df \tag{13}$$

where, $K(fr) = \frac{Z(fr)}{\sum_{fr} Z(fr)}$ and $K(fr) = \frac{Z(fr) = \left|F\left[{}_{Pre}I^{Aud}(t)\right]\right|}{\sum_{fr} Z(fr)}$

Thereby, the extracted audio features are represented as $ft_3 = \left[f^{emd}, f^{spec}\right]$.

3.7 Serial-based Maximum Information Feature Fusion (S-MIFF)

The feature fusion step is a critical phase in multimodal sentiment analysis, where the features retrieved from multiple preprocessed modalities are combined to form a unified representation. The goal of feature fusion is to integrate the relevant information from each modality using an improved fusion technique that maximizes the model's capability to understand the sentiment. When combining the features, there is a risk of including redundant information. Redundant features don't add value and conventional method include irrelevant features. So, to overcome this, this work presents a serial based maximum information with correlation function [40].

Let consider ft_1 , ft_2 and ft_3 be the three text, image, and audio feature vectors, respectively. Then the serial based fusion is defined as in Eq. (14).

$$SF(v) = \begin{bmatrix} ft_1 \\ ft_2 \\ ft_3 \end{bmatrix} \tag{14}$$

Although this method integrates all three features into a single matrix, the results indicate that many of the fused features contain irrelevant details. To tackle this challenge, a new technique known as the serial-based maximum information feature fusion process has been developed. This process first computes Principal component analysis (PCA) [41] to each feature to address the issue dimensionality variations in feature. The PCA approach helps to reduce high-dimensional data by comparing other two feature set while preserving important variance.

For example, $ft_1 = [1, 2,3,5,8]$, $ft_2 = [0, 4,6,7,10]$and $ft_3 = [5,7,8,11,3]$ are the three feature set. Apply PCA to these features to balance the dimensionality. Then, the balanced fused serial matrix is formulated as in Eq. (15).

$$SF\ (v) = \begin{bmatrix} 1 & 2 & 3 & 5 & 8 \\ 0 & 4 & 6 & 7 & 10 \\ 5 & 7 & 8 & 11 & 3 \end{bmatrix} \tag{15}$$

Further, compute the maximum information as in Eq. (16) and it obtains the maximum information in matrix format as, max $=[5\ 7\ 8\ 11\ 10]$.

$$M = \max\left(SF\ (v)\right) \tag{16}$$

Then, compare this maximum information matrix format with each feature as in Eq. (17), Eq. (18) and Eq. (19)

$$v_1 = compare\ (ft_1, M) \tag{17}$$

$$v_2 = compare\ (ft_2, M) \tag{18}$$

$$v_3 = compare\ (ft_3, M) \tag{19}$$

This will compares each feature with maximum information; if the matrix format of maximum information and the feature set has same value, it retains that number; otherwise, represented as 'zero'. Thereby, it provides the output vector as $v_1 = [0 \quad 0 \quad 0 \quad 0 \quad 0]$ $v_2 = [0 \quad 0 \quad 0 \quad 0 \quad 10]$ and $v_3 = [5 \quad 7 \quad 8 \quad 11 \quad 0]$ Moreover, compute correlation between each vector and consider C be the correlated value. The correlation is computed between two different vectors as $C_1\ (v_1, v_2)$, $C_2\ (v_1, v_3)$ and $C_3\ (v_2, v_3)$. By using correlation, it can further eliminate redundant features that don't add value, which leads to more efficient representation of data. Then, compute the average of these correlations as defined in Eq. (20). Finally, merge these correlation values with each vector as in Eg.(21)

$$C = Avg\ (C_1, C_2, C_3) \tag{20}$$

$$Sff\text{max} = (v_1 * C) + (v_2 * C) + (v_3 * C) \tag{21}$$

Thus, the proposed approach combines the best information of both deep models. The maximum information approach ensure that only the most relevant features are retained.

3.8 Hybrid sentiment analysis model

A hybrid sentiment analysis model combines machine learning and lexicon-based approaches to leverage the strengths of both. While machine learning models excel at pattern recognition and adaptability, lexicon-based methods offer interpretability and domain-specific sentiment scoring. This fusion enhances accuracy, robustness, and generalizability across diverse datasets and languages.

In the Hybrid sentiment analysis model, the fused features *Sff*max obtained from serial based maximum information are subjected to hybrid sentiment analysis model that involves two classifiers like Position Attention Module assisted LeNet (PAM-LNet) and SqueezeNet, as shown in Figure 3. These classifiers trains the features, *Sff*max and the intermediate of these scores are exposed to take average to obtain the final sentimental predictions as '0' for Negative, '1' for Positive and '2' for Neutral. The description and architecture of these two classifiers are described as follows:

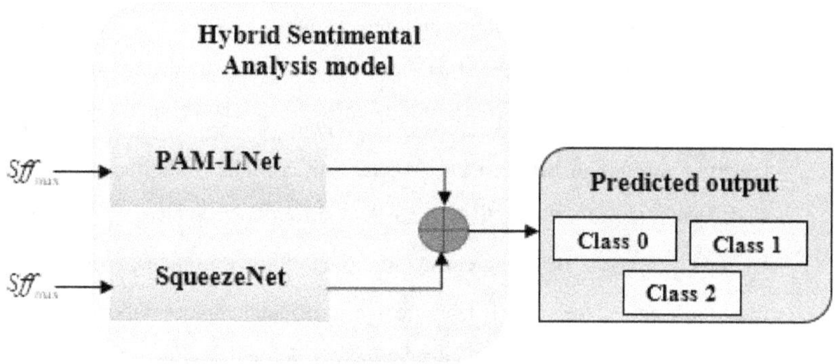

Figure 3.5: Flow of Hybrid Sentimental Analysis

3.8.1 Position Attention Module assisted LeNet (PAM-LNet)

The Position Attention Module assisted LeNet is the variant of LeNet [42] model that is a convolutional neural network that performs very well in sentimental prediction. However, it is relatedly shallow architecture with only a few layers. Its effectiveness is limited when appear to high dimensional and more complicated data. Also, it was designed with fixed input dimension. To address this, PAM-LNet model is introduced that improves the network stability during training. The proposed PAM-LNet architecture processes the fused feature through multiple stages to extract and refine features before classification. Initially, the input (fused feature) passes through a 1x1 convolutional layer, which helps in dimensionality reduction while preserving important spatial information. This is followed by an average pooling layer that reduces spatial dimensions and a Leaky ReLU activation to introduce non-linearity. Additionally, the processed features then go through a 3x3 convolutional layer, which captures local patterns, followed by another average pooling layer for further down-sampling. A sigmoid activation function is applied to control the range of feature values, followed by a dropout layer to prevent over-fitting. Figure 4 shows the Structural representation of PAM-LNet.

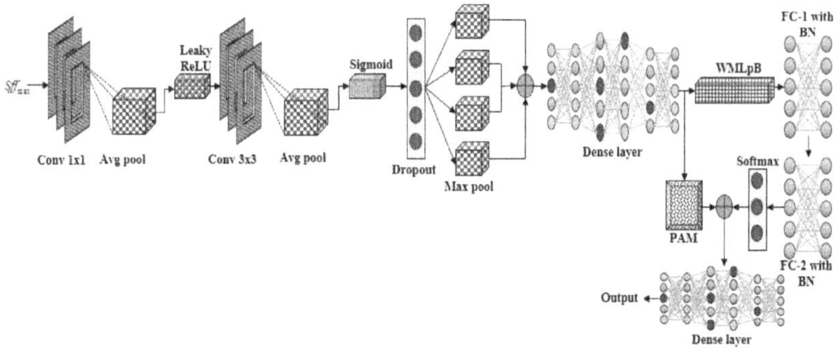

Figure 3.6: Structural Representation of PAM-LNet

The architecture then branches into four parallel max pooling layers, which extract key features at different levels. These outputs are concatenated, merging diverse spatial features into a single representation. The concatenated feature map is then subjected to a dense layer, followed by Weighted Mixed Lp-Batch normalization (WMLpB) to stabilize learning. The processed feature set moves to two fully connected layers (FC1 FC2), each followed by batch normalization, ensuring smoother gradient flow and better convergence. A softmax layer is applied for classification, producing probability distributions over classes. To enhance the final representation, the resultant from dense layer is passed into Position Attention Module (PAM) layer and then the network concatenates the output of the PAM and the output of the softmax layer, integrating both raw and probabilistic feature representations. This merged representation is passed through another dense layer, leading to the final output. This structured flow ensures robust feature Extraction, regularization, and improved classification accuracy.

Weighted Mixed Lp-Batch normalization: Initially, mixed and Lp pooling [43], B_j Formulation is computed as in Eq. (22). Then, apply weight to pooling layers as in Eq. (23) and then, perform batch normalization $b^{\wedge}$ [44]to the weighted pooling layer as in Eq. (24).

$$B_j = \left[\varphi \max_{i \in r_j} + (1-\varphi)\frac{1}{|r_j|}\sum_{i \in r_j} fv_i\right] + \left[\frac{1}{|r_j|}\sum_{i \in r_j} fv_i^Q\right]^{\frac{1}{Q}} \tag{22}$$

$$B_j' = \left[\ln\left(1+\left(\left|\ln\left(B_j\right)\right|\right)\right)\right] \tag{23}$$

$$\hat{b} = \left(\frac{b_i - \mu_B}{\sqrt{\sigma_B^2 + \varepsilon}} \right) * B_j ' \tag{24}$$

where, $\varphi = 1$; $Q > 1$; B_j indicates mixed-Lp pooling layer; fv_i denotes feature value at location i; r_j denotes pooling region; B_j' denotes weighted pooling layer; b_i denotes prior layer feature map; μ_B indicates mean of b_i, ε denotes constant and σ_B^2 refers to b_i.

Position Attention Module: The PAM [45] processes an input feature map of size $c \; \bar{h} \; w$ by generating three derived feature maps. Two undergo convolution, reducing their channels to $\frac{c}{8}$ and serve as query (Q), value (V) and key (K) to compute a spatial attention probability map, PAM_{Att} of size $(h \times w) \times (h \times w)$ as in Eq. (25). This spatial attention map helps aggregate relevant context while incorporating global semantics, ensuring intra-class consistency. The final prediction graph, PAM_f is obtained after reshaping the attention representation as in Eq.(26)

$$PAM_{Att} = soft\max\left(Q_{(hw \times c)} . K_{(c \times hw)}\right) \tag{25}$$

$$PAM_f = \left(V_{(c \times hw)} . PAM_{Att}\right).reshape\left(c \times h \times w\right) + Inp_{(c \times h \times w)} \tag{26}$$

Thus, the model is designed to be less sensitive to hyper parameter selection, ensuring easier and more effective training while preventing gradient vanishing.

3.8.2 Squeeze Net

Squeeze Net [46] is a lightweight deep learning architecture designed for efficient image classification, particularly aimed at reducing the model size while maintaining competitive performance. It achieves this by using a novel design principle called the fire module, which consists of two key components: "a squeeze layer and an expand layer". The squeeze layer practices 1x1 convolutions to diminish the input channels count, effectively compressing the feature maps. The expand layer then applies 1x1 and 3x3 convolutions to capture detailed information. This structure significantly diminishes parameters count and the computational demands, making Squeeze Net highly efficient compared to traditional deep learning models like Alex Net or VGG. Despite having fewer parameters, Squeeze Net achieves performance close to more complex models. Additionally, Squeeze Net employs strategies like early down sampling and global average pooling to further optimize its size and computational efficiency.

3.9 Summery

The research methodology for SqueezeNet centers on designing a deep learning architecture that drastically reduces model size while preserving high classification accuracy. The researchers began by identifying the limitations of existing models like AlexNet and VGG, which had large parameter counts and high computational demands. To address this, they introduced the fire module, a novel building block composed of a squeeze layer (using 1×1 convolutions to reduce input channels) and an expand layer (using 1×1 and 3×3 convolutions to capture rich features). This modular design was systematically tested and refined to minimize parameters without sacrificing performance.

The methodology also included strategies like early down sampling to reduce spatial dimensions early in the network and global average pooling to replace fully connected layers, further shrinking the model. The architecture was trained and evaluated on benchmark datasets like ImageNet, and its performance was compared against larger models to validate its efficiency and accuracy. Overall, the research followed a structured approach of problem identification, architectural innovation, experimental validation, and comparative analysis.

CHAPTER 4
EXPERIMENTAL SETUP

Experimental setup refers to the arrangement and configuration of all the components necessary to conduct an experiment. It's essentially the blueprint or framework that ensures the experiment is carried out in a controlled, repeatable, and scientifically valid way. Data Preparation and Preprocessing

4.1 Sentiment Analysis Classification Levels

Sentiment analysis classification levels refer to the different layers at which sentiment can be evaluated within a text. At the **document level**, the entire text is treated as a single unit, and the overall sentiment—positive, negative, or neutral—is determined. This is useful for understanding general opinions in reviews or articles. **Sentence-level analysis** breaks down the text into individual sentences, allowing for more precise detection of sentiment, especially in mixed-opinion content. **Aspect-level analysis** goes even deeper by identifying specific features or topics mentioned in the text and assessing sentiment toward each one—like evaluating the battery life versus screen quality in a phone review. Some advanced systems also perform **emotion-level analysis**, which detects nuanced emotions such as joy, anger, or sadness, offering richer insights into human expression. Together, these levels provide a comprehensive framework for understanding sentiment in natural language.

Sentiment analysis can be broadly categorized into three levels based on the granularity of the analysis:

4.1.1 Sentence-Level Analysis

At this level, each sentence is treated as an individual unit for sentiment evaluation.

Subjective sentences, which convey personal opinions or emotions (e.g., "Your saree color is too bright.") Objective sentences, which present factual information without expressing sentiment (e.g., "Most Indian women own a large collection of sarees.")

4.1.2 Document-Level Analysis

This approach considers the entire document as a whole to determine the overall sentiment. It assumes that the text reflects a unified opinion about a specific subject—such as a person, product, or place. Prior to sentiment classification, irrelevant or neutral sentences are typically filtered out to enhance accuracy.

4.1.3 Aspect-Level Analysis

Aspect-level sentiment analysis focuses on evaluating sentiments tied to specific features or components of an entity. A single opinion may address multiple aspects of the same item. For example, someone might find the color of a saree beautiful, but feel that its texture is disappointing.

4.2 Aspect Based Sentiment Analysis Taxonomy

Aspect Based sentiment analysis taxonomy with three aspects, Machine Learning approach, Hybrid approach, and Lexicon Based Approach. The taxonomy is shown in figure 4.1. We have experimented with rule-based and knowledge-based hybrid approaches which we call as Amalgam model. Aspect-Based Sentiment Analysis (ABSA) taxonomy categorizes the various approaches used to identify and evaluate sentiments tied to specific aspects or features within a text. This taxonomy helps researchers and developers understand the strengths and limitations of different models and choose the most suitable method for their application.

ABSA is a fine-grained sentiment analysis technique that goes beyond general sentiment classification by pinpointing specific aspects (e.g., "battery life" or "customer service") mentioned in a review or comment and determining the sentiment expressed toward each. The taxonomy of ABSA models is typically divided into three main categories: knowledge-based models, machine learning models, and hybrid models.

Knowledge-based models rely on predefined rules, sentiment lexicons, and ontologies to extract and classify aspect-related sentiments. These models are interpretable and easy to implement but may struggle with domain adaptation and ambiguity. Machine learning models, including traditional classifiers and deep learning architectures, learn patterns from labeled data and can generalize better across domains. They often use techniques like Support Vector Machines (SVM), Conditional Random Fields (CRF), or neural networks to detect aspects and sentiments. However, they require large annotated datasets and may lack transparency. Hybrid models combine the strengths of both approaches, using rule-based systems to guide or enhance machine learning predictions, thereby improving accuracy and adaptability.

This taxonomy also considers the granularity of aspect extraction—whether aspects are predefined categories (e.g., "food", "service") or dynamically discovered from the text. Additionally, it includes models that handle implicit aspects, sarcasm, and multi-aspect sentences. As ABSA continues to evolve, this structured taxonomy provides a roadmap for developing more robust and context-aware sentiment analysis systems.

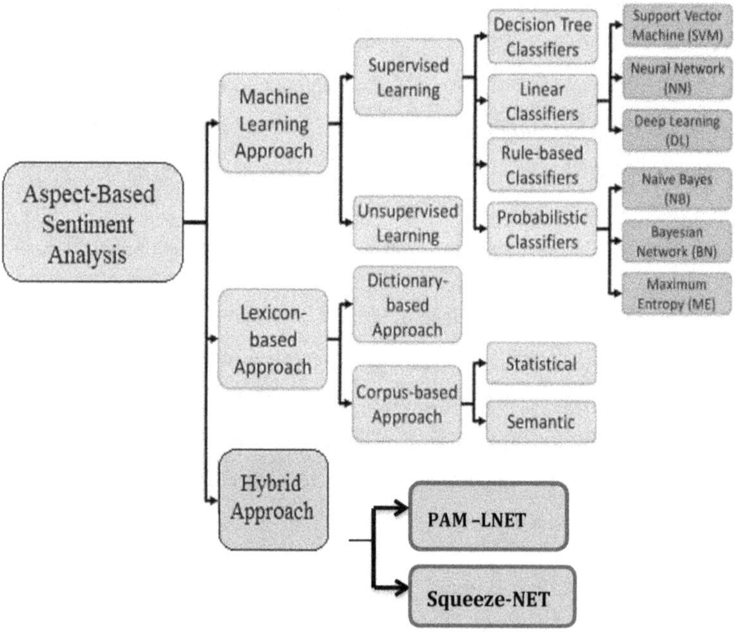

Figure 4.1: Aspect Based Sentiment analysis Taxonomy

4.2.1 Approaches in Aspect-Based Sentiment Analysis (ABSA)

Aspect-Based Sentiment Analysis employs several core methodologies to identify and evaluate sentiments tied to specific aspects within text. These include:

- **Knowledge-Based Approaches**: These rely on sentiment lexicons and domain- specific resources to assign polarity scores to aspect-related terms. They are particularly effective in low-resource settings where annotated data is scarce.
- **Rule-Based Approaches**: These use manually crafted linguistic rules and syntactic patterns to detect aspect terms and infer sentiment. Such systems often incorporate dependency parsing and part-of-speech tagging to analyze sentence structure and sentiment flow.
- **Machine Learning Approaches**: These involve training classifiers on labeled datasets to predict sentiment for identified aspects. Techniques like Support Vector Machines (SVM) or Naive Bayes are commonly used, requiring feature engineering to capture aspect-sentiment relationships.
- **Deep Learning Approaches**: These leverage neural networks such as LSTM, CNN, or transformer-based models to automatically learn complex patterns between aspects and sentiments. They excel in capturing contextual nuances and handling implicit sentiment expressions.

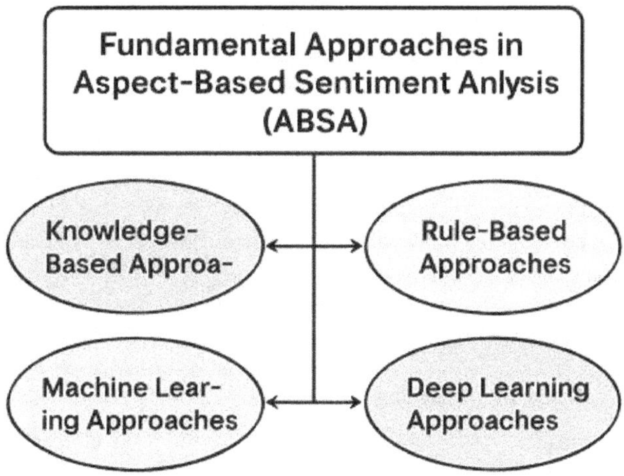

Figure 4.2: Approaches for ABSA

4.2.2 Data Preparation and Preprocessing

Use benchmark datasets like Twitter-2015, Twitter-2017, or SemEval ABSA datasets that include both text and image pairs annotated with aspect-level sentiment labels[2][1].

Ensure datasets contain diverse aspect terms and sentiment polarities across modalities. Preprocessing plays a vital role in multimodal sentiment analysis pipeline. In order to ensures uniformity across data from different sources (text, image, audio), making it easier to integrate and analyze. Let assume $I\ Txt$, $I\ Img$, and I^{Aud} be the input text, image and audio, respectively. As each modality has distinct features, the preprocessing steps for each modality are discussed as follows.

4.2.3 Text preprocessing

Text data, typically contains noise, irrelevant words, and inconsistencies. The preprocessing for text aims to clean and standardize the data for further investigation. The common steps involved are as follows:

Tokenization: Tokenization [28] is the process of dividing a sentence into distinct tokens, such as words or symbols, and is achieved through the split () method. For example, the sentence-"The movie was absolutely amazing with great performances and a compelling storyline" will be splitted into tokens as 'The', 'movie', 'was', 'absolutely', 'amazing', 'with', 'great', 'performances', 'and', 'a', 'compelling', and 'storyline'. This output is fed into the further stemming process.

Stemming: Stemming is a technique employed in pre-processing to strip suffixes from words, find their base form, reduce the word count, and save both memory and time. The stemming process is applied to the above tokens and obtain the stemmed output as 'The', 'movie', 'was', 'absolute', 'amaze', 'with', 'great', 'performance', 'and', 'a', 'compel', and 'storyline'.

4.2.4 Image preprocessing

Images, I^{Img} need to be processed to eliminate noise, adjust brightness/contrast, and enhance important features before feature extraction. In this work, the input image, I^{Img} is preprocessed using Gaussian filtering technique.

Gaussian filtering: Gaussian filtering [29] is a technique, which is used to reduce noise and smooth images or signals.To reduce noise in image inputs, a Gaussian filter was employed. It works by applying a Gaussian function to I^{Img}, where each point in I^{Img} is weighted based on its distance from the center. The two dimensional Gaussian filtering is formulated as in Eq. (1).Here, σ^2 refers to variance.

$$Gaus(p,q)=\frac{1}{2\pi\sigma^2}e^{-\left(p^2+q^2\right)/2\sigma^2} \tag{1}$$

Thus, the preprocessed image is denoted as ${}_{Pre}I^{Img}$.

The preprocessing for text aims to clean and standardize the data for further investigation.

In the preprocessing stage, a Gaussian filter was applied to images for noise reduction, where the average value of the kernel over a given range was computed by discretizing the continuous Gaussian function into a finite kernel window and normalizing the weights so that they sum to one. This normalization ensures that the filter preserves overall image intensity while effectively smoothing local variations, thereby maintaining structural integrity in the data. To validate correctness, the implementation was verified against pre-computed values for small sigma Gaussians, confirming that the discretization and normalization process produced accurate and reliable filtering results.

4.2.5 Audio preprocessing

Audio data, I^{Aud} is highly susceptible to noise and inconsistencies. Preprocessing helps to clean I^{Aud} and extract the relevant features for sentiment analysis using the Low-pass filtering approach

4.3 Feature extraction

Feature extraction plays a vital role in multimodal sentiment analysis by transforming pre-processed inputs—such as text, images, and audio—into structured representations that deep learning models can effectively utilize for sentiment classification. This step emphasizes isolating the most relevant information from each modality, enabling the model to gain a deeper understanding and more accurate interpretation of the data across different formats. The goal is to distill each modality into its most informative components: for text, this might include syntactic and semantic features like word embeddings or sentiment-bearing phrases; for images, visual cues such as facial expressions, color tones, or scene context; and for audio, prosodic features like pitch, tone, and rhythm that convey emotional nuance. By extracting these features, the model can capture the unique sentiment signals embedded in each modality and integrate them for a more holistic understanding of user emotion. Advanced techniques like convolutional neural networks (CNNs) for image features, recurrent neural networks (RNNs) or transformers for text, and spectrogram analysis for audio are commonly employed. Effective feature extraction not only enhances model accuracy but also enables cross-modal alignment, allowing the system to reconcile conflicting signals and deliver more nuanced sentiment predictions features that deep learning models can use for sentiment classification. This process focuses on identifying the key information within each modality, allowing the model to better understand and interpret the data.

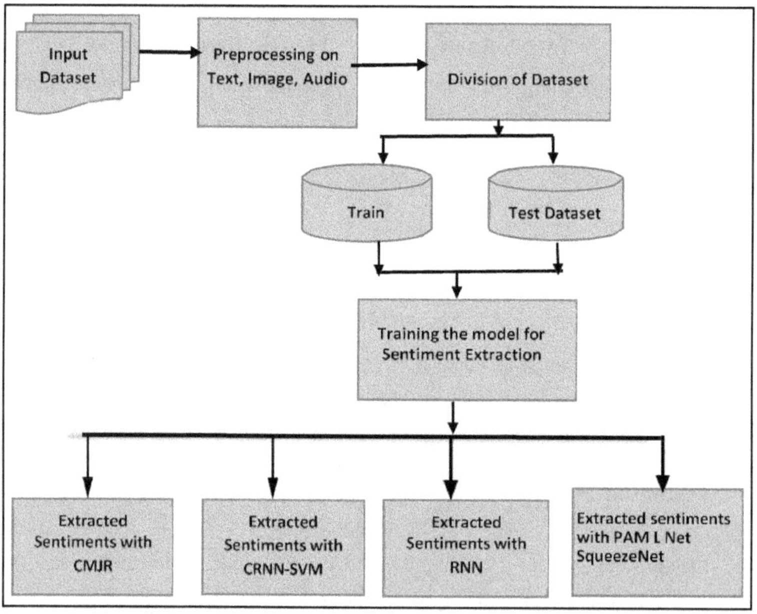

Figure 4.3: Sentiment Extractions with Popular Approaches

4.3.1 Image feature extraction

For the preprocessed image I_{Img}, the feature extraction process focuses on identifying visual patterns, shapes, textures, and other characteristics that are relevant for sentiment analysis are discussed in the following:

PHOG: Pyramid Histogram of Oriented Gradients [36] represents an image at various resolutions using HOG features and spatial information from local segments. The image is divided into multiple areas at distinct resolutions, and segments are squared along axes to form increasing spatial grids. The sum of points in four cells at each level represents the pyramid structure.

LGIP: The LBP feature works by comparing the intensity of each pixel with its 8 neighboring pixels, assigning 8 binary bits, which are then converted into a Decimal label, as represented in Eq. (11).

$$lbp\ (y_c, z_c) = \sum_{x=0}^{7} l(I_x - I_c) \tag{11}$$

Where, $l(s) = \begin{cases} 0, & s \geq 0 \\ & s < 0 \end{cases}$: I_c denotes intensity of central pixel; and I_c denotes intensity of xth neighbor.

4.3.2 Audio feature extraction

Audio data requires specific techniques to capture important features related to tone, pitch, rhythm, and other acoustic characteristics that convey sentiment. Some common feature extraction methods for audio include:

EMD: EMD [38] f_{emd} serves as an efficient method for analyzing non-linear and non-stationary data, frequently applied in speech signal processing. It decomposes a given signal into several oscillatory modes determined as Intrinsic Mode Functions (IMFs) along with a residue, as indicated in Eq. (12).

$$Emd\ (c) = \sum_{i=1}^{n} H_i(t) + R_n(t) \tag{12}$$

where, $R_n(t)$ denotes residue and $H_i(t)$ indicates Intrinsic mode function.

4.3.3 Video feature extraction

Video feature extraction is a crucial step in data processing that involves identifying and isolating meaningful attributes from video content to facilitate analysis, classification, or prediction tasks. These features can include visual elements such as motion vectors, object shapes, colors, and textures, as well as audio cues and temporal patterns across frames. By converting raw video data into structured representations—like frame-level descriptors, optical flow, or deep learning embeddings—feature extraction enables efficient indexing, retrieval, and interpretation of video datasets. This process is widely used in applications such as surveillance, activity recognition, video summarization, and multimedia search, where understanding dynamic visual information is essential for intelligent decision-making.

4.4 Hybrid sentiment analysis model

In the Hybrid sentiment analysis model, the fused features Sff_{max} Obtained from serial based maximum information are subjected to hybrid sentiment analysis model that involves two classifiers like Position Attention Module assisted LeNet (PAM-LNet) and SqueezeNet, as shown in Figure 3. These classifiers trains the features, Sff_{max} and the intermediate of these scores are exposed to take average to obtain the final sentimental predictions as '0' for Negative, '1' for Positive and '2' for Neutral. The description and architecture of these two classifiers are described as follows: The hybrid sentiment analysis framework leverages fused features derived through a serial-based maximum information strategy.

These enriched features are then processed through a dual-classifier architecture comprising **Position Attention Module-enhanced LeNet (PAM-LNet)** and **SqueezeNet**. Each classifier independently learns and interprets the input representations, generating intermediate prediction scores. These scores are subsequently averaged to produce the final sentiment classification, where the output labels are defined as:

- **0** – Negative sentiment
- **1** – Positive sentiment
- **2** – Neutral sentiment

The structural design and operational mechanisms of PAM-LNet and SqueezeNet are detailed in the subsequent sections, highlighting their individual contributions to the overall model performance.

Table 4.1: Dual-stream hybrid sentiment classification system

Stage	**Description**
Input Layer	Two parallel inputs labeled Sff_max represent the fused feature vectors.
Classifier Branches	Each input is fed into a separate deep learning model: PAM- LNet and SqueezeNet.
Feature Processing	Both models extract and learn high-level representations from the input data.
Fusion Node	Outputs from PAM-LNet and SqueezeNet are merged using an averaging mechanism.
Prediction Output	The final sentiment class is determined based on the averaged scores:
	- Class 0: Negative - Class 1: Positive - Class 2: Neutral

This architecture exemplifies a **hybrid deep learning approach**, combining spatial attention mechanisms with lightweight convolutional networks to enhance sentiment prediction accuracy. Python was mentioned as the implementation tool, a baseline algorithm should be explicitly presented. In this case, the baseline could be a single-modal sentiment classifier (e.g., text-only TF-IDF + SVM, or image-only PHOG + CNN).This baseline provides a reference point to demonstrate the improvement achieved by the proposed multimodal PAM-LNet-MSA framework. TF-IDF vectors combined with a conventional machine learning classifier such as Support Vector Machine (SVM). This approach represents a widely used static text-level sentiment analysis method, which does not incorporate multimodal cues or advanced attention mechanisms. While effective in capturing coarse sentiment patterns, the baseline algorithm typically suffers from lower accuracy due to its inability to exploit complementary information from audio and visual modalities.By contrasting the results of this baseline with the proposed PAM-LNet-MSA multimodal framework, the improvement in accuracy, precision, and F-measure can be clearly demonstrated. The baseline thus serves as a benchmark reference, highlighting the added value of multimodal fusion and position attention in achieving fine-grained sentiment analysis.

4.5 Dataset Description

This dataset meticulously explained with labels for "subjectivity, sentiment intensity, per-frame and per-opinion visual features, and per-millisecond audio features." In addition, it comprises baseline outcomes for upcoming investigation and an innovative multimodal fusion method that cooperatively investigates spoken words and visual gestures. The Raw folder was systematized into 3 distinct directories like "Audio, Transcript, and Video"—each with dual sub-directories. For our investigation, the total of 3159 data instances were utilized, classified into three distinct classes like Negative (Label 0), Positive (Label 1) and Neutral (Label 2). Before augmentation process, the dataset comprised 1023 instances in the Negative class, 1080 instances in the Positive class and 96 data samples in the Neutral class. After the augmentation process, the Negative and Positive class remained unchanged at 1023 and 1080, while Neutral class increased to 1056 instances.

Table 4.2: Sample Text and Pre-processed Text

Sample Text	Pre-processed Text
"OK BUT THE TWO BIG CHARACTER APPEARANCES IN THIS MOVIE ARE EASILY DEADPOOL AND GAMBIT	ok but the two big charact appear in thi movi are easili deadpool and gambit
MY REASON IM A COMIC BOOK FAN	my reason im a comic book fan
STRANGE SINCE ONE OF MY BIGGEST GRAPES WITH THE XMAN SERIES WAS AND ALWAYS IS THE XXX	strang sinc one of my biggest grape with the xman seri wa and alway is the xxx"

4.6 Comparative Assessment

A comprehensive evaluation was conducted to analyze the performance of the PAM-LNet+SqueezeNet framework in comparison with existing methodologies. This study employed a diverse set of performance metrics—including Sensitivity, Negative Predictive Value (NPV), Specificity, F-measure, False Negative Rate (FNR), Precision, False Positive Rate (FPR), Matthews Correlation Coefficient (MCC), and Accuracy—to rigorously assess the effectiveness of the proposed strategy. In addition to these metrics, Receiver Operating Characteristic (ROC) curve analysis, Ablation studies, and Statistical evaluations were performed to ensure a robust and multidimensional validation. The PAM-LNet+SqueezeNet approach integrates principles from both machine learning and deep learning paradigms. While traditional machine learning classifiers such as Support Vector Machines (SVM) and CRNN-SVM were used for comparative analysis, the study also benchmarked against advanced deep learning architectures including RNN, DenseNet, EfficientNet, SqueezeNet, and LeNet. Furthermore, comparisons were drawn with cutting-edge models like CMJRT [26], highlighting the competitive edge of the proposed hybrid framework.

All models were evaluated using the CMU-MOSI dataset, a widely recognized benchmark for sentiment analysis, ensuring the reliability and generalizability of the results. The findings underscore the superior performance and adaptability of the PAM-L Net + SqueezeNet scheme across a range of evaluation criteria.

4.7 Ablation Study

An ablation study describes where certain features of the structure are eradicated to gain a better comprehension of the overall system's behavior. The ablation assessment on PAM-LNet-MSA strategy in contradiction to discrete variants such as PAM-LNet-MSA with Existing Aspect Term, PAM-LNet-MSA with Existing Feature Fusion, PAM-LNet-MSA with Improved LeNet and PAM-LNet-MSA with LeNet+SqueezeNet for Multimodal Sentiment Analysis is illustrated in table 4. The PAM-LNet-MSA employing Existing Aspect Term and PAM-LNet-MSA with Existing Feature Fusion acquired the F-measure scores of 0.831 and 0.888, while the PAM-LNet-MSA with Improved LeNet and PAM-LNet-MSA with Existing LeNet+SqueezeNet accomplished slightly improved F-measures of 0.902 and 0.908. However, the PAM-LNet-MSA strategy achieved the highest F-measure value of 0.935, suggesting that it provide superior performance compared to other variants.The FPR acquired using the PAM-LNet-MSA model is 0.032, indicating lesser error value. In contrast, PAM-LNet-MSA with Existing Aspect Term, PAM-LNet-MSA with Existing Feature Fusion, PAM-LNet-MSA with Improved LeNet and PAM-LNet-MSA with LeNet+SqueezeNet demonstrated greater FPR values ranging from 0.105 to 0.067. Therefore, it indicates that the PAM-LNet-MSA with all the improvements like DL-ATE, S-MIFF and PAM-LNet makes the overall system more effective in multimodal sentiment classification.

Table 4.3: Ablation Analysis on PAM-LNet-MSA Model, PAM-LNet-MSA with Existing Aspect Term, PAM-LNet-MSA with Existing Feature Fusion, PAM-LNet- MSA with Improved LeNet and PAM-LNet-MSA with LeNet+Squeeze Net

	PAM-LNet-MSA with Existing Aspect Term	PAM- LNet-MSA with Existing Feature Fusion	PAM- LNet-MSA with Improved LeNet	PAM-LNet-MSA with Existing LeNet+ SqueezeNet	PAM-LNet-MSA
MCC	0.766	0.853	0.878	0.883	0.902
FPR	0.105	0.076	0.074	0.067	0.032
Specificity	0.895	0.924	0.926	0.933	0.968
FNR	0.170	0.112	0.098	0.093	0.066
Precision	0.831	0.888	0.902	0.908	0.936
NPV	0.895	0.923	0.926	0.932	0.967
Sensitivity	0.830	0.888	0.902	0.907	0.934
Accuracy	0.874	0.912	0.918	0.924	0.956
F-measure	0.831	0.888	0.902	0.908	0.935

CHAPTER 5
RESULT AND DISCUSSION

Researchers found that untrained attention mechanisms often misalign with human intuition, leading to unreliable explanations. However, when attention is guided by human-annotated rationales, not only does model performance improve, but the interpretability of predictions also becomes more faithful and transparent.

5.1 Procedure

The Proposed Fine-Grained Multimodal Sentiment Analysis was simulated using PYTHON ("Version 3.7"). The processor utilized was "AMD Ryzen 5 3450U with Radeon Vega Mobile Gfx 2.10 GHz and the Installed RAM size was 16.0 GB". Further, the Multimodal Sentiment Analysis was conducted using CMU-MOSI [47].

5.2 Dataset Description

This dataset meticulously explained with labels for "subjectivity, sentiment intensity, per-frame and per-opinion visual features, and per-millisecond audio features." In addition, it comprises baseline outcomes for upcoming investigation and an innovative multimodal fusion method that cooperatively investigates spoken words and visual gestures. The Raw folder was systematized into 3 distinct directories like "Audio, Transcript, and Video"—each with dual sub-directories.

For our investigation, the total of 3159 data instances were utilized, classified into three distinct classes like Negative (Label 0), Positive (Label 1) and Neutral (Label 2). Before augmentation process, the dataset comprised 1023 instances in the negative class, 1080 instances in the Positive class and 96 data samples in the neutral class.

After the augmentation process, the Negative and Positive class remained unchanged at 1023 and 1080, while Neutral class increased to 1056 instances.

5.3 Performance Analysis

The comprehensive analysis was performed to assess the performance of PAM- LNet+SqueezeNet approach in comparison to extant methodologies. This investigation employed a wide range of performance measures, such as "Sensitivity, Negative Predictive Value (NPV), Specificity, F-measure, False Negative Rate (FNR), Precision, False Positive Rate (FPR), Matthews Correlation Coefficient (MCC), and Accuracy," to determine the effectiveness of PAM- LNet+SqueezeNet strategy. Moreover, the ROC Curve analysis, Ablation Study and Statistical Analysis were conducted. Further, the PAM-LNet+SqueezeNet strategy is compared with state-of-the-art methods like CMJRT [26] and CRNN- SVM [27], as well as traditional classifiers like RNN, DenseNet, EfficientNet, SqueezeNet and LeNet. The PAM-LNet+SqueezeNet scheme and conventional methodologies were evaluated utilizing the CMU-MOSI Dataset, validating a robust estimation and validation of the results.

5.3.1 Pre-processing Analysis

Figure 16 showcases the original signal images alongside its consistent LPF using pre-processed images for Audio signal data. The LPF is employed to eliminate high-frequency noise. Figure 17 displays the original video images together with their resultant Gaussian filtering images for Video Data. The Gaussian Filter is utilized to remove noise. Table 2 presents the Sample Text with its preprocessed outcomes, attained through the combination of Tokenization and Stemming, demonstrating the text data preprocessing process.

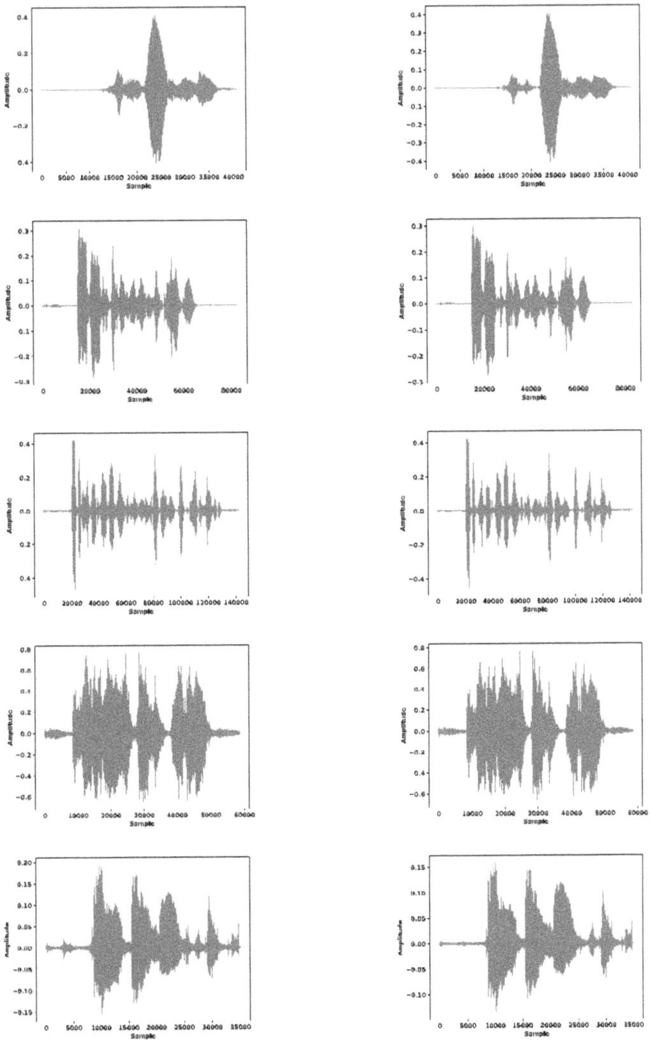

(a) (b)

Figure 5.1: Pre-processed Image Results for Audio Signal Data a) Sample Audio Signals and b) LPF using Pre-processed signals

(a) (b)

Figure 5.2: Pre-processed Image Results for Video Data a) Sample images and b) Gaussian Filter using Pre-Processed images

5.4 Comparative Assessment

In the quest of Multimodal Sentiment Analysis, an exhaustive analysis was conducted to compare the performance of PAM-LNet+SqueezeNet strategy with conventional methods like CMJRT [26], CRNN-SVM [27], RNN, DenseNet, EfficientNet, SqueezeNet and LeNet. This section investigates the performance of these models, specifically focusing on their capability to categorize the sentiments by analyzing the Positive, Negative and Neutral measures. The findings are presented in figure 16, figure 17 and figure 18. For a system to be considered effectual, its necessities to attain larger positive and neutral measure scores, indicating its efficiency in accurately identifying and categorizing different emotions. For 60% training data, the PAM-LNet+SqueezeNet strategy attained the highest accuracy score of 0.918, which surpasses the state-of-the-art approaches like CMJRT [26] (0.805) and CRNN-SVM [27] (0.811). Also, it outperforms the conventional classifies, including RNN (0.859), DenseNet (0.863), EfficientNet (0.834), SqueezeNet (0.885) and LeNet (0.868). As the training data enhances to 70% and 80%, the accuracy of the PAM-LNet+SqueezeNet approach improves to 0.929 and 0.954, surpassing the conventional methods. Finally, with 90% training data, the PAM-LNet+SqueezeNet approach demonstrated the greatest accuracy of 0.956, while CMJRT [26], CRNN-SVM [27], RNN, DenseNet, EfficientNet, SqueezeNet and LeNet exhibited lesser accuracies, ranging from 0.881 to 0.930. When compared to the conventional approaches, it signifies that the PAM-LNet+SqueezeNet scheme provides a higher level of precision values. The PAM-LNet+SqueezeNet scheme has a precision rate of 0.932 in 80% training data, significantly surpassing the established methodologies. In the DCNN-AM model performed well in training process to diminish the amount of parameter adjustments. The weight adjustment procedure in FC layer can be decreased suggestively, which emphasis the learning of convolutional layer.

For 70% training data, the PAM-LNet+SqueezeNet scheme exhibited the highest NPV rate of 0.947, whereas the conventional approach scored lesser NPV values with CMJRT [26] at 0.868, CRNN-SVM [27] at 0.893, RNN at 0.906,

DenseNet at 0.900, EfficientNet at 0.893, SqueezeNet at 0.921 and LeNet at 0.903, respectively. Similarly, the PAM-LNet+SqueezeNet model generated better values compared to conventional schemes in terms of F-measure and MCC. The Negative measure ratings should be minimalized for effective categorization of emotions. While analyzing the negative metric analysis, the PAM-LNet+SqueezeNet strategy outperforms the conventional methods. In particular, the PAM-LNet+SqueezeNet approach attained the least FNR of 0.070 at the training data 70%, though the CMJRT [26], CRNN-SVM [27], RNN, DenseNet, EfficientNet, SqueezeNet and LeNet scored greater FNR values. When trained with 90% data, the PAM- LNet+SqueezeNet model achieved the minimal error score of 0.066, again surpassing the conventional strategies. Among these, the CMJRT [26] and CRNN-SVM [27] recorded higher FNR values of 0.180 and 0.161, indicating worst performance. The DenseNet and EfficientNet generated the FNRs of 0.145 and 0.155, while RNN, LeNet and SqueezeNet exhibited scored the error values of 0.139, 0.110 and 0.106. This indicates that the PAM-LNet+SqueezeNet model has the ability to classify the emotions. The S-MIFF technique combine the best information of features from the three modalities. The maximum information approach confirms that only the most applicable features are retained.

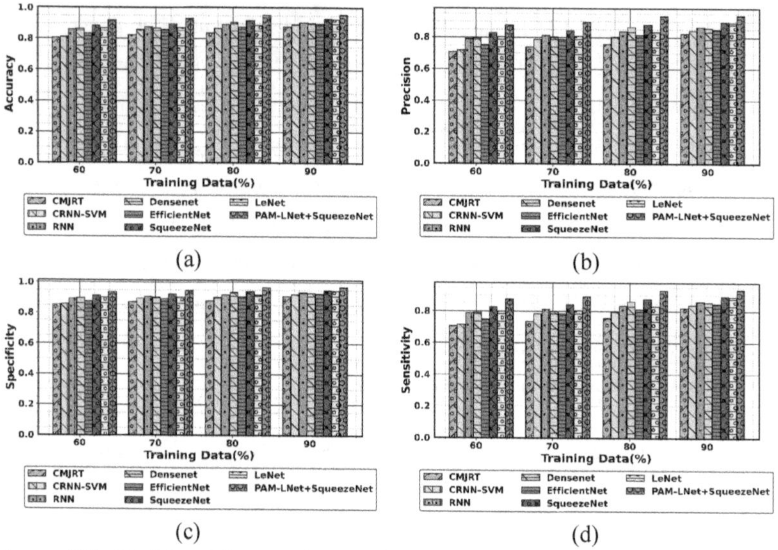

Figure 5.3: Positive Measure Evaluation of PAM-LNet+SqueezeNet Versus Traditional Methodologies a) Specificity b) Sensitivity c) Accuracy and d) Precision

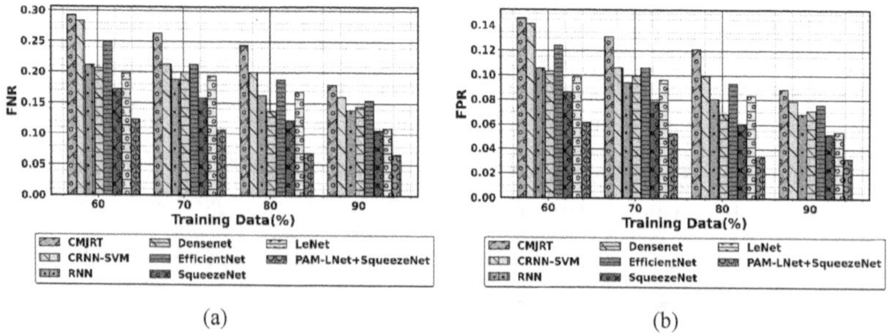

Figure 5.4: Negative Measure Evaluation of PAM-LNet+SqueezeNet Versus Traditional Methodologies a) FNR and b) FPR

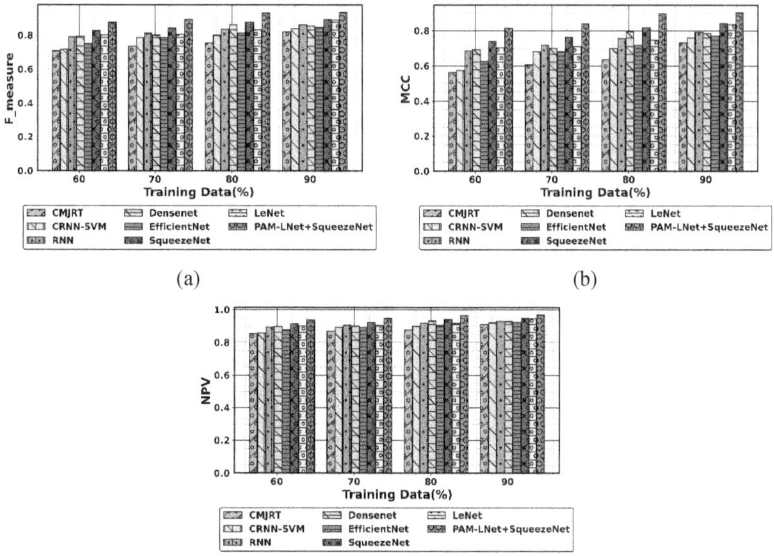

(a) (b)

(c)

Figure 5.5: Neutral Measure Evaluation of PAM-LNet+SqueezeNet Versus Traditional Methodologies a) F-Measure b) MCC and c) NPV

5.5 Analysis on ROC Curve

The ROC Curve is a visual illustration of model performance across each thresholds. In Figure 21, the ROC curve analysis on PAM-LNet+SqueezeNet approach is compared with conventional methods, including CMJRT [26], CRNN-SVM [27], RNN, DenseNet, EfficientNet, SqueezeNet and LeNet for Multimodal Sentiment Analysis. The PAM-LNet+SqueezeNet accomplished the peak AUC rate of 0.953, suggesting excellent discrimination in accurately categorizing various emotion states. Comparatively, the traditional approaches like CMJRT [26], CRNN-SVM [27], RNN, DenseNet, EfficientNet, SqueezeNet and LeNet demonstrated lesser AUC values, which ranges from 0.785 to 0.947. By using Correlation in S-MIFF system can further eliminate redundant features that don't add value, which leads to more efficient representation of data.

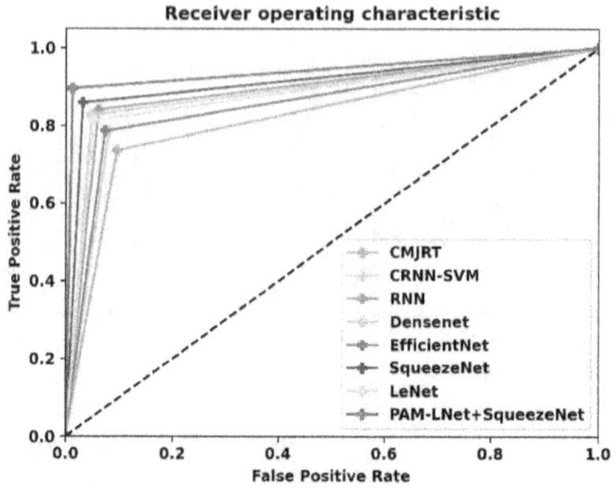

Figure 5.6: ROC Curve Evaluation on PAM-LNet+SqueezeNet versus Conventional Methods

5.6 Statistical Analysis on Accuracy

Table 8 explains the comprehensive statistical assessment on PAM-LNet+SqueezeNet methodology in comparison to existing approaches like CMJRT [26], CRNN-SVM [27], RNN, DenseNet, EfficientNet, SqueezeNet and LeNet for Multimodal Sentiment analysis. Regarding Maximum Statistical Metric, the PAM-LNet+SqueezeNet achieved the peak accuracy of 0.956, suggesting its exceptional performance in precisely categorizing different emotion states. As compared this performance with conventional strategies like CMJRT [26], CRNN-SVM [27], RNN, DenseNet, EfficientNet, SqueezeNet and LeNet, which demonstrated reduced accuracy values ranging from 0.881 to 0.930. Additionally, the greatest accuracy value is attained using the PAM-LNet+SqueezeNet approach is 0.942, whereas the CMJRT [26], CRNN-SVM [27], RNN, DenseNet, EfficientNet, SqueezeNet and LeNet exhibited the accuracies of 0.831, 0.862, 0.883, 0.885, 0.867, 0.907 and 0.879, respectively. The inclusion of WMLpB in PAM-LNet, which enhances the stability of network and faster convergence during training. Reduce the sensitivity to the choosing of hyperparameter, becoming the model simpler to train successfully. Moreover, it benefits to evade gradient vanishing problem.

Table 5.1: Statistical Evaluation on Accuracy

Statistical Metrics	CMJ RT [26]	CRNN- SVM [27]	RNN	Dense Net	Efficient Net	Squeeze Net	LeNet	PAM-LNet+SqueezeNet
Minimum	0.805	0.811	0.859	0.863	0.834	0.885	0.868	0.918
Mean	0.837	0.857	0.884	0.886	0.866	0.907	0.888	0.939
Standard Deviation	0.028	0.030	0.018	0.021	0.023	0.018	0.024	0.016
Median	0.831	0.862	0.883	0.885	0.867	0.907	0.879	0.942
Maximum	0.881	0.893	0.908	0.909	0.898	0.930	0.927	0.956

The final PAM-LNet-MSA model consistently outperforms all other configurations across nearly all metrics, highlighting the synergistic benefits of its combined components. For instance, its Accuracy is the highest at 0.956, significantly better than "PAM-LNet-MSA with Existing Aspect Term" (0.874), "PAM-LNet-MSA with Existing Feature Fusion" (0.912), "PAM-LNet-MSA with Improved LeNet" (0.918), and "PAM-LNet-MSA with Existing LeNet+SqueezeNet" (0.924).

Looking at the Matthews Correlation Coefficient (MCC), a balanced measure of performance, the PAM-LNet-MSA model achieves the highest score of 0.902. This indicates a strong correlation between its predictions and the actual sentiment labels, surpassing the 0.766 of "Existing Aspect Term," 0.853 of "Existing Feature Fusion," 0.878 of "Improved LeNet," and 0.883 of "Existing LeNet+SqueezeNet." In terms of error rates, the PAM-LNet-MSA model demonstrates the lowest False Positive Rate (FPR) at 0.032 and False Negative Rate (FNR) at 0.066, signifying fewer incorrect positive and negative classifications respectively. This is a considerable improvement compared to other configurations, which exhibit higher FPRs (e.g., 0.105 for "Existing Aspect Term") and FNRs (e.g., 0.170 for "Existing Aspect Term").

The PAM-LNet-MSA model also achieves the highest Specificity (0.968) and Negative Predictive Value (NPV) (0.967), indicating its superior ability to correctly identify negative instances and that a negative prediction is truly negative. Furthermore, its Precision (0.936), Sensitivity (0.934), and F-measure (0.935) are all the highest among the configurations, demonstrating its robust performance in correctly identifying positive instances and achieving a good balance between precision and recall. In summary, the ablation analysis clearly illustrates that each enhancement integrated into the PAM-LNet-MSA model—from improved LeNet architecture to specialized feature fusion and aspect term handling—contributes incrementally to its superior overall performance, ultimately resulting in a highly effective sentiment analysis model.

5.7 Comparison on PAM-LNet-MSA and Unimodal Methods

Table 5.2: PAM-LNet-MSA and Unimodal Methods

Aspect	**PAM-LNet-MSA (Multimodal)**	**Unimodal Methods (Text/Image/Audio Only)**
Data Modalities	Integrates text, image, and audio for richer emotional context	Relies on a single modality—typically text
Sentiment Accuracy	Higher accuracy due to cross-modal reinforcement and attention mechanisms	Moderate accuracy; may miss emotional cues not present in the chosen modality
Noise Reduction	Uses multi-hop attention and position-aware filtering to suppress irrelevant signals	Limited ability to filter noise, especially in noisy text or ambiguous audio
Interpretability	Attention maps highlight sentiment-relevant regions and timeframes across modalities	Interpretation is modality-dependent and often less transparent
Context Sensitivity	Captures nuanced emotional expressions like sarcasm, tone, and facial cues	May misinterpret context due to lack of multimodal input
Computational Complexity	Higher due to multimodal fusion and attention modules	Lower; faster to train and deploy
Domain Adaptability	Well-suited for domains like healthcare, education, and social media	Effective in structured domains but less robust in emotionally rich environments
Real-Time Feasibility	Requires optimization for real-time use due to heavier architecture	Easier to deploy in real-time systems

PAM-LNet-MSA excels in capturing the full spectrum of human emotion by combining multiple modalities and applying position-aware attention, making it ideal for complex, real-world sentiment tasks.

Unimodal methods, while simpler and faster, often fall short in understanding nuanced emotional expressions, especially when sentiment is conveyed through tone or visuals. For example, a sarcastic comment like "Great job!" paired with a frustrated facial expression and harsh tone would likely be misclassified by a text-only model but correctly interpreted by PAM-LNet-MSA. The comparative evaluation of PAM-LNet-MSA Scheme is relative to unimodal cases, including Text, Audio and Video for the investigation of sentiments is exposed in table 6. This analysis underlines the performance difference among the PAM-LNet-MSA multimodal system and to each of the unimodal strategies. In table 5, the PAM-LNet-MSA method exhibited superior performance compared to the unimodal approaches. Specifically, the PAM-LNet-MSA scheme achieved the highest specificity rate of 0.968, while unimodal methods scored lesser specificities with 0.943 for Text, 0.951 for Audio and 0.936 for Video. The DCCN-AM is employed to extract the aspect features. Further, the S-MIFF approach ensure that the most appropriate features are retained. The PAM-LNet and SqueezeNet are utilized to refine sentiment predictions. By incorporating these methodologies, the PAM-LNet-MSA model exhibited improved performance in multimodal sentiment analysis.

Table 5.3: Evaluation on PAM-LNet-MSA Versus Unimodal Approaches

Metrics	Unimodal-text	Unimodal-audio	Unimodal-video	PAM-LNet-MSA
Accuracy	0.935	0.942	0.929	0.956
F-measure	0.920	0.927	0.915	0.935
FPR	0.057	0.049	0.064	0.032
Specificity	0.943	0.951	0.936	0.968
Precision	0.920	0.927	0.915	0.936
Sensitivity	0.919	0.926	0.914	0.934
FNR	0.081	0.074	0.086	0.066
NPV	0.942	0.950	0.936	0.967
MCC	0.897	0.903	0.894	0.902

The comparative analysis table highlights the performance of various sentiment analysis models across different modalities, including Unimodal-text, Unimodal- audio, Unimodal-video, and the proposed PAM-LNet-MSA framework. Among these, PAM-LNet-MSA consistently delivers superior results across nearly all evaluation metrics, underscoring its effectiveness in handling multimodal sentiment data. Specifically, it achieves the highest **accuracy** at 0.956, surpassing Unimodal- text (0.935), Unimodal-audio (0.942), and Unimodal-video (0.929). In terms of **F- measure**, PAM-LNet-MSA again leads with 0.935, followed closely by Unimodal- audio (0.927), while Unimodal-text and video trail behind at 0.920 and 0.915 respectively. The model also excels in **precision** and **sensitivity**, scoring 0.936 and 0.934, indicating its strong capability to correctly identify both positive and negative sentiments. Furthermore, PAM-LNet-MSA records the lowest **False Positive Rate** (0.032) and **False Negative Rate** (0.066), reflecting minimal misclassification. Its **specificity** (0.968) and **Negative Predictive Value** (0.967) are the highest among all models, reinforcing its reliability. Although the **Matthews Correlation Coefficient** (MCC) shows a minor discrepancy—0.902 for PAM-LNet-MSA versus 0.903 for Unimodal-audio the overall performance clearly favors. In the preprocessing stage, the Gaussian filter was applied not only as a smoothing kernel but also with consideration of convolutional parameters that influence its behavior. Padding was used to ensure that the filter could operate at the edges of images without discarding boundary information, thereby preserving facial features that are often critical for sentiment cues. The stride parameter controlled the step size of the kernel sweep, with a stride of one chosen to guarantee that every pixel contributed to the smoothed output, maintaining fine-grained detail essential for accurate sentiment recognition. Although less common for Gaussian filters, dilation was conceptually acknowledged as a mechanism to expand the receptive field by introducing gaps within the kernel, allowing broader contextual patterns to be captured if required. Together, these parameters demonstrate that the Gaussian filter is not a static tool but a configurable operation whose design choices directly affect the quality of feature preservation and noise reduction in multimodal sentiment analysis.

While the Gaussian filter in preprocessing is primarily used for static image denoising, its behavior is also shaped by convolutional parameters such as padding, stride, and dilation, similar to those employed in deep learning architectures. In Gaussian filtering, padding ensures that edge pixels are included in the smoothing process, preventing the loss of boundary information that may carry sentiment cues in facial expressions. Stride determines the step size of the kernel sweep; a stride of one is typically chosen to guarantee that every pixel is smoothed, whereas larger strides reduce computational cost but risk overlooking fine details. Dilation, though less common in Gaussian filters, can be conceptually applied to expand the receptive field by introducing gaps in the kernel, allowing broader contextual patterns to be captured. In contrast, convolutional filters within deep learning models such as PAM-LNet use these parameters dynamically to balance local detail and global context during feature extraction.

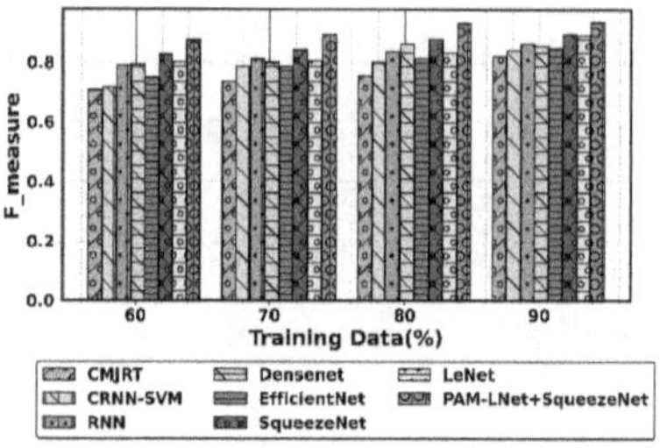

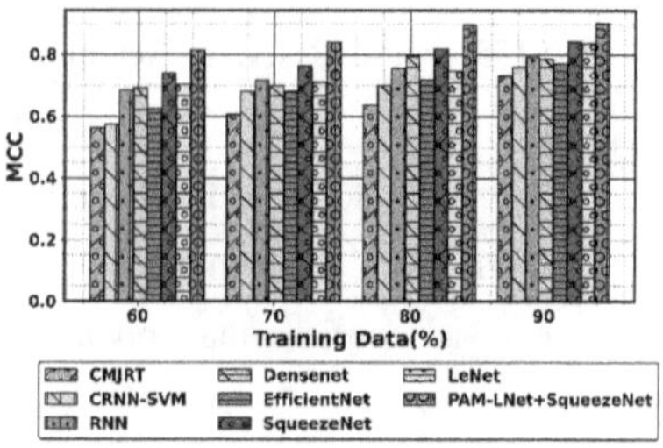

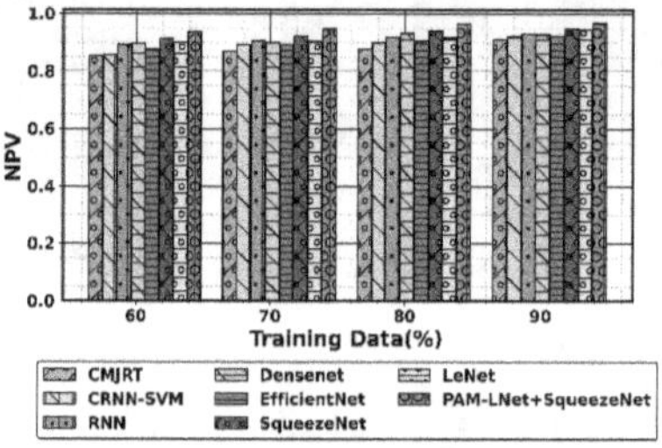

CHAPTER 6

CONCLUSION AND FUTURE WORK

Conclusion and Future Scope

Endings are the best part; they give hope for new beginnings."

— Elle Sommer

Research, by nature, is an ever-evolving and limitless pursuit. However, within the framework of doctoral studies, it adheres to a structured trajectory. Every Ph.D. investigation is expected to culminate in a definitive conclusion, encapsulating its key achievements and discoveries.

In this chapter, we provide a succinct overview of the primary contributions and insights derived from our research efforts. Following this, we examine the limitations encountered during the study and outline potential avenues for future inquiry. Subsequently, we delve into the constraints we encountered and the prospects for future exploration. Finally, in research publications and presentations, we shed light on the significant milestones we encountered throughout this journey.

6.1 Research Contributions

The essence of research lies in an unwavering curiosity, a drive to address real- world challenges, and a strong ethical compass. It thrives on the conviction that innovation and discovery can spark meaningful transformation. Far from static, research is a fluid and continually progressing endeavor—one that deepens our grasp of the world and empowers us to improve it in impactful ways. With this thought, we have tried to predict aspect based sentiment analysis for multimodal data with multiclass classification with the help of Machine Learning and Deep Learning Modal

This study introduced a novel multimodal sentiment analysis framework, PAM- LNet-MSA, designed to effectively process and integrate data from text, image, and audio sources. The preprocessing phase ensured modality-specific noise reduction and normalization, while the feature extraction phase utilized advanced techniques such as DL-ATE and TF-IDF for text, PHoG and LGIP for images, and EMD with spectral features for audio. These features were unified using the S-MIFF fusion strategy, enabling a comprehensive representation of multimodal data.

The fused features were then analyzed using a hybrid deep learning architecture combining PAM-LNet and SqueezeNet, which demonstrated superior performance in sentiment classification. With 60% training data, the proposed model achieved an impressive accuracy of 0.918, outperforming both state-of-the-art methods like CMJRT [26] **and** CRNN-SVM [27], as well as conventional classifiers including RNN, DenseNet, EfficientNet, SqueezeNet, **and** LeNet.

These results validate the effectiveness of the PAM-LNet-MSA framework in capturing nuanced sentiment patterns across multiple modalities, highlighting its potential for real-world applications in emotion-aware systems, multimedia analysis, and human-computer interaction.

6.2 Conclusion

In our framework, the sentiment unit is treated as a configurable output dimension that adapts to the labeling scheme of the dataset. For example, in CMU-MOSI, the sentiment unit can be binary (positive/negative) or continuous (-1 to $+1$), while CMU-MOSEI employs a multi-valued unit on a seven-point scale, and MELD extends this to multi-class emotions. Similarly, CH-SIMS provides continuous sentiment values suitable for regression-based units. This flexibility demonstrates that the PAM-LNet-MSA model is not restricted to a single sentiment representation but can be tuned to binary, multi-valued, or continuous units depending on dataset requirements. By explicitly acknowledging sentiment unit control, we highlight the adaptability of our framework and its capacity to capture both coarse polarity and fine-grained emotional intensity, thereby strengthening its relevance across diverse multimodal sentiment analysis applications.

The configuration of the sentiment unit directly aligns with the labeling schemes of different multimodal datasets, allowing the model to adapt its output granularity to the task at hand. In the case of CMU-MOSI, sentiment can be represented either as a binary unit, distinguishing between positive and negative polarity, or as a continuous unit, capturing fine-grained intensity values in the range −1 to +1. By contrast, CMU-MOSEI employs a multi-valued sentiment unit with a seven-point scale, enabling nuanced distinctions across varying degrees of positivity and negativity, while datasets such as MELD extend this approach to multi-class emotion categories. Similarly, CH-SIMS provides continuous sentiment values, making it suitable for regression-based sentiment units. This flexibility demonstrates that the PAM-LNet-MSA framework is not restricted to a single sentiment representation but can be tuned to binary, multi-valued, or continuous units depending on dataset requirements, thereby enhancing its adaptability and relevance across diverse multimodal sentiment analysis applications.

The process began with the input phase, where data from text, images, and audio were processed. For text, the process involved tokenization and stemming. The images were filtered via Gaussian filter to remove noise, while audio was cleaned using a low-pass filter to eliminate high-frequency noise. The next phase was feature extraction, where the system extracted key features from each modality. For text, DL-ATE and TF-IDF were extracted. Images were analyzed using PHoG and LGIP. For audio, EMD and spectral features captured the frequency patterns of the sound. After extracting features, the system integrating the features from all three modalities using a S-MIFF approach. This unified set of features was then passed to a sentiment analysis model, where advanced deep learning architectures like PAM-LNet and SqueezeNet were employed to refine sentiment predictions. For 60% training data, the PAM-LNet+SqueezeNet strategy attained the highest accuracy score of 0.918, which surpasses the state-of-the-art approaches like CMJRT [26] (0.805) and CRNN-SVM [27] (0.811). Also, it outperforms the conventional classifies, including RNN (0.859), DenseNet (0.863), EfficientNet (0.834), SqueezeNet (0.885) and LeNet (0.868).

6.3 Future Scope

A promising direction for future work lies in extending multimodal sentiment analysis toward dynamic system modeling, where sentiment is treated not as a static label but as a time-varying state that evolves across sequences of text, audio, and visual cues. In this context, the Kalman filter offers a principled approach for estimating hidden emotional states by recursively updating predictions with new observations, thereby accounting for noise and uncertainty inherent in multimodal data streams. Such a framework would enable the system to track sentiment trajectories in real time, smoothing abrupt fluctuations while preserving meaningful transitions. Dynamic system models combined with Kalman filtering could also enhance robustness in noisy environments, improve temporal coherence in sentiment predictions, and support applications such as conversational agents, adaptive learning platforms, and affective computing systems. By integrating these techniques, future research can move beyond static classification toward continuous, context-aware sentiment tracking, opening pathways for more responsive and human-like multimodal analysis.

While the proposed model has shown promising results, several avenues remain open for future exploration:

- **Dataset Expansion**: Applying the framework to larger and more diverse datasets could further validate its generalizability and robustness.
- **Real-Time Implementation**: Optimizing the model for real-time sentiment detection in live multimedia streams could enhance its practical utility.
- **Cross-Lingual and Cross-Cultural Analysis**: Extending the model to handle multilingual and culturally diverse data would broaden its applicability.
- **Explainability and Interpretability**: Incorporating explainable AI techniques could help users understand the decision-making process behind sentiment predictions.
- **Integration with Social Platforms**: Embedding the model into social media monitoring tools or customer feedback systems could provide deeper insights into public sentiment.